To: Barbara

ANGEL NIGHTINGALE

A Nurse's Journey of Healing With Angels

Love,

Soodabeh Mokry, RN ,CHt

Certified Hypnotherapist
Certified Angel Intuitive Practitioner

BALBOA.
PRESS

A DIVISION OF HAY HOUSE

Balboa Press books may be ordered through booksellers or by contacting:

Balboa Press
A Division of Hay House
1663 Liberty Drive
Bloomington, IN 47403
www.balboapress.com
1 (877) 407-4847

Print information available on the last page.

ISBN: 978-1-5043-5228-4 (sc)
ISBN: 978-1-5043-5230-7 (hc)
ISBN: 978-1-5043-5229-1 (e)

Library of Congress Control Number: 2016904758

Balboa Press rev. date: 06/07/2016

In order to protect the confidentiality of my family and clients, their names, genders, cities and states they are from, and other identifying information have been changed to protect their identities. The stories are more than eighteen years old, and the majority of my clients have transitioned to the spirit world. It was an honor to serve them while they were in their physical forms!

ACKNOWLEDGMENTS

I dedicate this book to my grandparents, my father, and my
brother, who are my guardian angels in the spirit world.
To my mother, who loved me unconditionally and tried
her best to make sure her children had a better life.
To my brothers, niece, and nephews, I love you so much
and I am very proud of each and every one of you.
To my teachers, coaches, and mentors Bruce Terrill
and Renee Madsen Terrill, who taught me the best
way to live, always connected to the divine spirit.
To my editor, Kristin Thiel, thank you for your
loving nature, wisdom, and guidance.
And to my clients and their families, who accepted me
by opening their homes and their hearts and who have
been the best part of this journey and transition.
Thank you!

PART 1

LIFE IN IRAN

CHAPTER 1

I sensed that the man before me was not sleeping but dead, yet all I could see was his thinning hair—beautiful, dark wisps over a shiny scalp. I longed to touch them. I began to feel I *had* touched them, that I intimately knew their curl, the stubbornly flat spots, and the way the hands of the man fussed with them. I had seen those hands, that hair, that fussing in my bathroom mirror. My husband. "Hameed!" I screamed and fell toward this dead man.

I sat up. A murmur from my lap oriented me. I was holding Azeeta, my two-year-old daughter. We were in the two-bedroom house my two kids, my two brothers, my mother, and I shared in Iran. Azeeta settled and stayed asleep, and I stood up to put her to bed. I heard the constant blare of car horns and vendor calls outside the window, which was open in a weak effort to circulate the steaming August air. It was late afternoon, and I'd fallen asleep after working a busy shift in the university hospital and taking two buses each way for the privilege.

I went into the kitchen to make dinner. Cyrus, my six-year-old son, was playing with his toys in the living room, talking to them as if they could really hear him, bursting into laughter at times.

"Cyrus, could you please be quiet? Azeeta is sleeping."

He started walking toward me, his smiling black eyes making me smile. "Good, I am hungry," he said. What are you making?"

"Chicken with rice, your favorite. Do you want to help me?"

Nodding, Cyrus turned and ran out of the kitchen, returning a moment later carrying his toys—red, gold, black, and blue Matchbox cars. While he played with them, he told me stories from day care. I tried to listen and interact with him while making food.

I washed the white basmati rice and put it on the stove. Then I started to fry the chicken, stirring herbs and spices such as turmeric, saffron, salt, and pepper into the pan. The aroma of the spices and olive oil made Cyrus impatient.

"I am so hungry, Mom." His little hands rubbed his stomach, but he kept smiling. "I am really hungry! When can I eat?"

"Soon, honey. We have to wait for Grandma, Uncle Soheil, and Uncle Seamak to come home before we eat. Do you want some milk and cookies?"

Cyrus agreed to a snack and went back to playing with his cars, moving them back and forth and in a circle, talking to them. I was trying to listen to him, but his voice would fade at times as I was trying to make sense of my dream. The image of the dead man haunted me.

Could he really have been Hameed? I thought. *Oh God, is he okay?* I wished I could pick up the phone and call him. I missed him so much—his touch, the sound of his laughter, the way he used to play with Cyrus like he too was a kid. Tears filled my eyes, but I wiped them with my sleeve; I refused to cry in front of Cyrus.

Hameed had fled Iran three years before to set up a new and better life in America for our children and me. We talked on the phone only once a month. It was very expensive, and I couldn't afford it, even though I was working six days a week. He was living with his sister in America, working part-time and going to school, barely making enough money to survive.

I heard Cyrus again, asking questions. "Mom, did you hear me?" He pulled my skirt with his little hand, trying to get my attention. "Mom, why don't you answer me?"

"I am sorry, honey. I heard you. I am listening to you and trying to get the food ready. Tell me the story. What happened after that?"

My mom and brothers came home later that evening, and we ate dinner. Although I couldn't get the awful image of the dead man who looked too much like my husband out of my head, I decided not to discuss that with anyone.

Cyrus chattered away. "I helped Mom make dinner today," he repeated, feeling very proud of his accomplishment. "Mom, is Uncle Soson coming to visit tonight?"

My mom looked at him and said, "Your Uncle Soson and Aunt Seema and Ali went to Rasht to see the new baby. Aunt Seema's sister has a new baby girl. Do you remember? They are there to visit."

Cyrus and I spoke at the same time.

"When are they coming back? I want to play with Ali," he said, missing his three-year-old cousin.

"I didn't know he went there. I just talked to him yesterday, and he didn't tell me he was going there." I said. A knot of anxiety started to grow in my stomach. "He promised me he was going to go get his passport ready to take us to Turkey."

My brother was planning to take us to the American Embassy in Turkey, so my children and I could get visas to go to America. A year and a half year younger than I, he assumed the role of protector while Hameed was in America. He had always been very thoughtful, taking care of everyone—not just my kids and me. He even called my mom every day, making sure she was okay.

My mom answered Cyrus first. "Well, Ali and Aunt Seema are planning to stay there longer, but Uncle Soson was planning to come back this morning." She turned to me and said, "I don't know why he didn't tell you—maybe he forgot. He is really busy with work, I guess. He has to make sure everything is ready before Seema has their baby." Mom paused, and a curious look crossed her face. "He didn't call me today."

"Maybe he was too busy with work and travel and just forgot," I said, teasing her. I was being purposefully casual, echoing what she had just said to me.

"Too busy to call his mother?"

I laughed, and soon she cracked a smile.

We ate our dinner and watched TV until I was tired. I had to get up early in the morning to go to work.

"Okay, Cyrus. Say goodnight."

Sometime later, I heard my mom sobbing. I wasn't sure if it was a dream or not. I opened my eyes, lifted my head off the pillow, and tried to pay attention. It was real. I got up, opened the door gently, closed it just as gently behind me to not wake up the kids, and walked to the living room. Mom was sitting on the floor, crying. Soheil and Seamak were sitting right in front of her on the floor holding her hands, trying to calm her down. They both looked like they had just woken up, looking disheveled in their pajamas, staring at my mom with eyes wide open.

Her short gray hair couldn't hide the tears running down her cheeks. "He is not back yet. He is not back yet. I know something is wrong. Nobody knows where he is. I know something is wrong." She could barely get the words out.

"Mom, what are you talking about? I don't know what you are saying. You need to calm down. I don't understand you."

Hearing me, she gathered herself and wiped her tears from her cheeks. "I am talking about Soson. Seema called me, asking if I had heard anything from him yet. She said Soson hasn't called her since he left Rasht early this morning."

It was unlike Soson not to call his wife or my mom after coming back from a trip. I felt sick in my stomach, thinking about the dream I had earlier.

Crying again, my mom continued, "He should have been here before noon. It's only a five-hour drive from Rasht."

I was praying quietly. "Oh, dear God, please help him wherever he is—just keep him safe."

Soheil started pacing the room, and Seamak dropped his head into his hands. Their faces were red, yet they were trying not to show any emotions, being more concerned about keeping Mom calm than sharing their own feelings.

Mom got up to get the phone. She called one of our cousins to find out if he had heard anything from Soson yet.

"Soson has been missing, and no one has heard anything from him. I am terrified of what might have happened to him. Maybe he was in a car accident. Call the hospitals and the police department to see if they have any idea," Mom told our cousin before she hung up the phone.

"I knew it. I had a bad feeling today. I didn't want to do anything or go anywhere. I knew it. Where could he be? Oh God, I can't live without my baby," Mom said, bursting into tears again.

Every second seemed like hours as we waited to hear some news of hope. I was sitting on the floor, leaning on the living room floor, leaning against the wall, unable to drive away the thought of my dream. I continued to cry and pray quietly.

The sound of the phone ringing shook me to attention. Mom rushed to answer it. It was our cousin. He told her he had news, so she put him on speakerphone. "Soson was in a car accident early this morning," he said. "He is in the hospital and waiting to have surgery in the morning. I think it would be a good idea to leave now, so you can get there in the morning before his surgery."

"I don't believe you. He must be dead. How come he didn't call us? He must be dead. Oh my God, my son is gone!" Mom screamed in one breath.

I was speechless, still trying to balance my dream with my cousin's words. Both felt like true versions of my brother.

Soheil called another cousin, who lived in town, and told him about Soson's accident.

"I am on my way. Don't worry about anything," Nader said. "I will drive and we'll get there before his surgery."

It was past midnight when we left Tehran to go to Rasht. It was a long drive—five hours in the darkness of night, and every minute seemed like forever.

"Look if you can see any signs of his white car. My baby had just bought his car," my mom said, gasping for air.

By the time we got to my aunt's house, it was morning. I saw my cousins standing by the red metal door, leaning against the brick wall, wearing black shirts and pants. The minute I saw their red eyes, I burst into tears, knowing that my nightmare had come true; I knew my brother was gone forever. I felt broken, shattered into pieces, and I couldn't take a step. I managed to get out of the car, but I fell onto the ground by the door, screaming.

"Oh, my God, no, no, no! Soson is gone! He is gone!"

My cousins helped me up and walked me to the house. "Come on, Soodabeh. Let's get inside." I saw that my aunt and the rest of the family were waiting for us. They came forward one by one to hold and comfort us. I could hear my mom howling in agony; everyone was crying and screaming in pain.

"Where is Seema?" my mom asked my aunt.

"She should be here soon with her mom. She doesn't know yet," my aunt responded.

Seema arrived shortly after, and the minute she saw us, her little body crumpled and fell. "Oh, God, oh, God, no. Please tell me he is okay. Oh, God, please." But she knew that her husband, the love of her life, was gone forever.

We had all unexpectedly lost someone—one of the most wonderful sons, brothers, fathers, cousins, and husbands we had ever known.

Soson had been in a car accident, but nobody knew exactly how it had happened. Even the police report was unclear about the cause of the accident. There were no other cars involved and no witnesses. All we knew was that when the police and paramedics arrived, he was alive. He had handed them his briefcase.

"Please give this to my family. There are important business documents inside this briefcase," he had said to a police officer. The police officer told my family, "He held his head and fell on the ground and became unconscious."

Soson was taken to the nearest hospital, but by the time they prepped him for surgery, he was gone.

Soson was a very kind, compassionate, and loving young man, only twenty-eight years old. He used to call my mom several times a day to see if she needed anything. He always made sure I had everything I needed. Soson used to buy lots of toys for Cyrus and spent time playing with him, so that he wouldn't miss his father.

"Why don't you come to live with me, Soodabeh? I'd feel more comfortable if you did. I want to make sure that you and the kids are taken care of," he used to say to me.

Soson was a wonderful husband and a loving father. He made sure that his family had everything. It was amazing that even after being thrown out of the car, he was thinking about his family. Giving the briefcase to the police officer, he made sure that his family would be safe. When we opened the briefcase, we found some checks and lots of important documents. His business partners knew that my brother was always thinking of the well-being of his family. As a result, they cashed the checks on his behalf and helped to buy a house for his wife and children.

I was very angry about the vision I had seen in my dream. "Why, God, did you show me my brother's death without telling me how to prevent it? What was I supposed to do with that?" I kept screaming in pain. I had been a nurse for many years. I had comforted so many people and saved so many lives. It was breaking my heart that I couldn't be there for my brother, to hold and comfort him and to save his precious life.

I couldn't stop crying and sobbing. Looking at his wonderful wife—seven months pregnant and with a three-year-old son—was making me crazy. I couldn't believe or accept my brother's death; it felt absolutely impossible for me to live and move on without him.

"Why did you take Soson? Why didn't you take me and both of my children instead?" I would ask God, but I couldn't hear any answers. I was miserable, angry with God, and didn't know how to find comfort dealing with such a horrific tragedy.

"Soodabeh, honey, you need to be patient. Please calm down," my family kept asking me. "You have to take care of your children. Think about them. They don't have their father here, and you are the only one they have. You have to be strong for your mother, Seema, and your children. Please calm down."

However, no matter what anyone said, nothing could take the pain away or comfort me. I would sob and cry from the time I woke up until the time I went to sleep.

I would dream about Soson, and I could hear his footsteps at nights. Sometimes I could even feel him by my bedside, touching my hair, and I would hear him talking to me. But of course I would wake up every time.

The day we had to bury him was the most difficult day of my life. The whole family came. His body was wrapped in a white sheet, a Muslim tradition, and he had a beautiful smile on his face; he looked very peaceful. My cousin came and held my hands, saying it was time for me to go and say good-bye to my brother.

"No, I can't. I don't want to. It should have been me. I can't go on without him. He was my younger brother. I should have died instead of him," I said. I was trembling, unable to walk or even to stand up.

"Why did you have to leave me? What am I supposed to do with your wife, with your son, with your unborn child? Who is going to take care of Mom?" I howled and howled in agony.

I didn't want to live, couldn't sleep, couldn't eat, and couldn't take care of my children. My mom and Seema were the same. It was nonstop crying, day and night. I don't know who took care of our children.

We went back to Tehran one week after the funeral. Knowing that I had to go back to work was making me frustrated and angry.

"I don't want to go back to work and take care of other people. I couldn't take care of my brother when he needed me. How can I do that for others?" I cried.

Thinking about what I had seen the day my brother died was confusing and painful. I kept asking myself the reason for that disturbing vision.

It was my first vision, and I was determined to make it the last one. In that moment of loss, I wasn't aware of the gift God had granted me. I had no idea that it marked the beginning of a new life. My brother had become an angel to guide me, awakening my spirit to pursue my life's purpose. I couldn't comprehend that the tragedy I had experienced would in turn lead me to follow my spiritual path, helping others to heal by finding peace and harmony.

CHAPTER 2

Though my entire family had lost someone special in Soson, and though we grieved together—I still felt alone. The love of my life was so far away from me, and we were not on good terms. I wasn't sure how I'd get through a phone call talking about Soson, but I knew I had to tell Hameed. He also needed to know, because he was expecting our children and me to be getting our visas soon; we were now very delayed.

The minute I started talking, tears started running down my face, my heart beat faster, and my body shook.

"I have bad news, Hameed. Soson … had … a … car accident … and … uh … " I said through my tears, but I couldn't continue. My cousin was sitting right beside me, holding my hand, trying to comfort me. I gave him the phone and burst into sobs, gasping for air. My cousin told Hameed.

In those moments, I'd had time to collect myself a little, enough for my mind to remember that the last time Hameed and I had spoken—the last few times—we had had only angry words for each other. As I took the phone back from my cousin, I wondered if Hameed would even still be on the line. He was.

"I don't know what to say, Soodabeh. How are you doing? How is Seema, the kids, your mom? Oh, my God. … how could this have happened? I can't believe it. I just can't," he said, mumbling. He became silent for a few seconds. Then he took a deep breath and said,

"I am so sorry. I don't know what to say—can't think or talk. Please take care of yourself. I will find a way to help you and the kids."

I hung up the phone and collapsed in sobs—for Soson, for my family, and for my marriage. I felt such despair, yet I also felt a warmth from Hameed's buoying words. But were they just a peak on the roller coaster? Or were we back on track?

I had met Hameed ten years before, after graduating from high school in September of 1978. At the time, I wasn't looking for a man; I was looking for a career. I was a hardworking student and had always wanted to be a doctor. However, I was unable to pass the entrance exam for medical school. There were too many applicants and not enough medical schools in Iran. Although I had high scores, it wasn't enough to be enrolled in the program. I was devastated when I found out.

"That's okay, honey. There are other things you can do. Not everyone could or should be a doctor," my mother had said.

"But I don't want to do anything else. I have always wanted to be a doctor! You know this!" I had told my mom, crying.

"Well, I know we will find a way. Don't worry about this for now. I am sure you'll figure it out soon."

A week later, my mom came home very excited. "Soodabeh, I have a great idea. How about you go to America to study medicine and come back home after you graduate? Lots of people have been doing this. What do you think?"

"Are you sure, Mom? How am I going to that? Who is going to pay? Where am I going to stay?" I asked. I was surprised and confused.

"Well, I know that your aunt loves you very much, and she would do anything to help. I am sure she would help us financially. It's just until you get your degree," she replied. "I think you should start taking classes to improve your English while we are working on your passport and visa."

I was nervous but very excited that my mom has decided to allow me to go to school in America. It was unbelievable and felt like a miracle!

My mom signed me up to take English classes at a local college. I had always loved speaking English and was very excited about becoming fluent. It was a scary thought— living in a different country without my family. But I was very happy, as it had been my dream to be a doctor since I was a little girl, and I was focusing on my English now, too.

It was an intense time for me to start making my way in the world. It was the beginning of the revolution in Iran. There were many political activists protesting every day and fighting for freedom and democracy. My mother was adamant about me not getting involved in any of those activities.

"Soodabeh, make sure to stay away from all this craziness. You are only to learn English—not to make friends or to get involved. Do you understand?" she demanded. She would take me to school and pick me up, making sure I was safe during that time, and—perhaps even more important to her—making sure I was attending class. My mother was a teacher, so school had always been important to her, but education became even more important after my father had died of a heart attack without warning when I was thirteen. Mom decided not to get remarried. Her focus was to raise us kids—my three brothers and me, the eldest—as best she could. That meant we needed to be well educated so we could get good jobs.

Hameed had been a student there too, with the same interest in learning English to move out of the country, though he wanted to be an engineer. However, he was also eager to understand what was going in Iran. He wanted democracy and was interested in getting involved in every protest and activity.

We started talking about what was going on in Iran, and slowly we became very good friends. Hameed reminded me of my father; he was very intelligent, loved books, and talked about everything. Although I didn't feel any chemistry or attraction at first, the fact that he reminded me of my father was very intriguing. I felt safe with him, able to talk about my feelings, my family, and my dreams. Although he was one year younger than me, he had graduated from high school the same year I did. Hameed was five feet nine and thin but muscular, with fine, short, black hair and a mustache and beard.

My mom had no idea about this friendship. I wasn't allowed to make any friends, just to do what I was expected to do: learn English!

After a few months, Hameed told me that he had started to have feelings for me. "Soodabeh, I really like you, and I was wondering if we can be more than just friends."

I had never had any boyfriends before; I hadn't been allowed to have any. I was expected to go to school, get a degree, find a job, and then get married to a man chosen by my parents.

I knew my mother would be really angry about Hameed, and after everything she had done for me, I had no intention of disrespecting her. My mother devoted her life to raising her children. She was working two jobs and had no social life. Besides, I knew that I would be leaving to go to America shortly; there was no point in making my life complicated. I had only one goal: to study to be a doctor.

"I don't think it is a good idea. I will be leaving soon, and so will you. I want to be able to go to school and be a doctor," I told Hameed.

"I have decided not to leave. I believe it would be a great idea for you to do the same," he told me. "We should stay and fight for our freedom. We deserve a better life here. Who is going to fight if we leave? We owe it to ourselves and our country," he insisted.

I wasn't sure about that at first, but he was very persistent. Eventually, after constant discussions, he convinced me that there would be a better life for us in Iran. I wanted to tell my mom, but I wasn't sure how she would react. How could I tell her that I had changed my mind? I knew she wouldn't like to hear about my decision at all.

"Mom, I don't want to go to America anymore. I don't know anyone there, and I'm not sure if I can survive. I want to go to college here. I will try to score high enough on the entrance exam next year. I promise I will study harder and take some extra classes. Please, Mom. Don't make me go."

Angel Nightingale

She stared at me for a few minutes and said, "Well, I think you can try. It would be easier for me to have you here in Iran with the family. It would be less worries and hard work for me," she said, smiling.

My mom was happy. I could see the light in her eyes, which made me feel relaxed and at ease. She knew that I wasn't really ready for the transition, since I had never lived alone. It would also be a financial burden for her if I went to America and much more affordable if I stayed and went to a local college in Iran.

Hameed and I were getting closer, and I thought it was time to share this with my mom. Although I knew it could make her upset, I was hopeful that she might appreciate my honesty and be open to accepting our relationship.

"Mom, I need to talk to you about something."

"What's going on? Is everything okay?"

"Well … umm …" I said, hearing my heart beating fast in my chest. "I met a very nice guy. His name is Hameed. We have been friends for a while, and I wanted to let you know," I said.

"Are you crazy? What will people think of you? I have worked so hard to make sure you have a great life, have education, find a great man to marry, and have a better future than mine. Why are you trying to throw everything away for a boy without any job or education? I forbid you to see or talk to him ever again. As a matter of fact, I forbid you to even go to that school anymore," she said, erupting like a volcano. "I have sacrificed so much, working very hard to put a roof over your head and making sure you have food to eat. All you need to do is to study and make sure you have good grades. That's not too much to ask, is it?"

But I had fallen in love and couldn't stop thinking about Hameed. Although I wasn't allowed to go to school, Hameed and I would see each other every day when my mom was working. We would talk on the phone for hours about anything and everything.

I studied hard and planned to pass the entrance exam for medical school the following year, but I failed again. As soon as my mom found out, she became extremely angry and agitated and started

15

pacing the floor. Then she got very close to me, staring into my eyes. She grabbed my shoulders and started shaking me.

"I can't believe this. How could you? I know it's all his fault. You could have done a better job if it wasn't for him. He is bad news. He is going to ruin your life and will leave you for someone else. You are wasting your time, Soodabeh. This is not acceptable, not at all," she said, repeating herself as she walked away. She slammed the door behind her and left the house.

One of my mom's cousins lived in Ahvaz, a city in the south of Iran that was very far from Tehran, where we lived. She was a nurse, and her husband was a prominent psychiatrist. My mom decided to send me there for nursing school.

"You shouldn't waste your life just because you can't go to medical school. You have to do something. You have to go to school to get an education to be able to take care of yourself. You know you can't depend on anyone else to take care of you. What would have happened to us if I wasn't a teacher? I had no idea that your father would die so soon. At least I can take care of us now. You have to do the same. You never know what life challenges you may face. You should have an education no matter what."

My mom was very independent and hardworking. She was strong and determined like a warrior, never afraid of anything or anyone. I had a lot of respect for her, and deep inside, I knew that she was right; I had to go to school. After a lot of thinking and soul searching, I decided that nursing was the best thing for me. Although it was very difficult to stay away from Hameed, I knew that it would be the best for me; we knew it was worth it.

"Soodabeh, I know nothing can come between us. I want you to succeed and be able to go to school and have a great career. It will be very hard, but I think this is the best thing for both of us. And knowing that I am saying this, maybe your mom will see that I am not a bad person, that I love you, and that I want the best for you after all," said Hameed, smiling.

I applied for nursing school, and I got accepted. My mom was very happy, I think as much about my future career as she was about my future love life. She thought Hameed and I would break up, and she'd be able to find the best man for me.

"I called your uncle, and he will travel with you to Ahvaz. He has already bought the tickets and will leave next week. It should be a great adventure for you, Soodabeh. I am sure you'll love it. I always wanted to be a nurse. Unfortunately, my father wanted me to be a teacher. I had to obey. I had no choice. Isn't that amazing that you have choices now?" my mom said.

"No, Mom. It isn't good. I always wanted to be a doctor, but now I have to settle down for less than I ever wanted and dreamed of. I am not even sure if I will like nursing. I don't think I have a choice either, Mom. I just don't!" I exclaimed with tears in my eyes.

It was hard not to have choices, but I also knew that this opportunity was not a bad one. I loved my uncle and was very excited that he was going to take me to Ahvaz. He had no idea about my relationship with Hameed and thought that I really wanted to be a nurse. It was my first time flying, and he made it a memorable trip, laughing and talking about our family.

"I am very proud of you, Soodabeh. You have grown up to be a young woman, able to go to college to be educated and independent. I couldn't have asked for a better niece. I hope you know that, my dear," my uncle told me. I was the first one in our family to go to college, and everyone was happy and proud of me.

I started the nursing program and was able to quickly make great friends. Mom would have been suspicious of that, but I kept my studies up too. I could do both. I kept calling Hameed and talking to him when my cousin wasn't home. I missed him terribly, but I was happy to be able to go to school. I knew that I was getting closer to my goal of being independent, able to take care of myself and have a great career.

And I will be able to get married and start a new life with Hameed soon, I thought.

Meanwhile, the Iranian government's craziness intensified. The government was making new rules about how to dress, walk, talk, and live. Police were arresting people for dressing differently, believing, thinking, or saying things we weren't expected to do or say. It was very scary, and we didn't know what to do.

We had been a Westernized country under the Shah, or king of Iran. We had freedom of speech, jobs, and religion. Men and women were equal, able to go to school, get an education, and be involved in politics. We were allowed to dress however we wanted. The new regime was making rules that were taking Iran back many centuries. No one was allowed to say anything against the government. We were all expected to obey the rules no matter what, or to accept jail and likely death as the consequences. Women were forced to dress differently, in long and wide dark pants and dresses, with no makeup, and with long black scarves to cover our hair. Men had to wear long-sleeve shirts, long pants, and grow beards. Women weren't allowed to go to law school or become a judge, and men were forbidden to be gynecologists. Our leaders were cruel and ruthless dictators.

Schools were forced to expel or fire students and teachers who didn't believe in the government's religious ideology. There was the threat of all schools being fully closed. A nationwide protest was scheduled; on the same day, all of the students and teachers all over Iran would protest.

"I am going to the university to attend the protest," Hameed told me. "What is the plan for you over there?"

"We are doing the same. I have my midterm exam, and after that I am going with some of my classmates."

My mom and cousin had no idea about my plan. They didn't think I would be bold enough to participate in the protests, thinking I was new in town and away from Hameed's influence. I had been good, going to school and coming home without any issues. There were no signs of me getting involved in anything but school. I thought that it wasn't necessary to let my cousin know about it, thinking that I would get home before she did.

Though we knew we were under threat, we were young; we didn't fully realize how serious things were. We had led good lives, so we expected good things in the end. We thought that the protest would be peaceful and swiftly successful, that a little chanting by us would make the government stop making decisions for all of us. After taking my test, I left the college with some of my classmates and went to the university.

I lounged on the stairs in front of the entrance to the university, talking with my friends, discussing the issues we had with the way things were going. We were so proud of ourselves for standing up to the government.

"We have to be strong. They have to learn that they can't just throw us out of school because we think or believe differently. We have to show them that we are determined to stand up for what we believe. We need freedom of speech and democracy. They can't treat us this way," said one of my classmates.

And then there were gunshots, one after another, followed by screaming. Everyone was terrified, running to find a safe place to hide, not knowing what had happened.

My friends and I found ourselves in the courtyard, but we were not safe there. We were quickly mobbed, surrounded by violent, angry men and women with guns, baseball bats, knives, and rocks. They hit us on our heads, arms, legs, and everywhere.

"You are all evil! You are sinners and deserve to die!" they screamed.

One of my friends took my hand and said, "Run, Soodabeh!"

Before we took another step, I felt a strong hand push me from the back, and I fell onto the cement. They continued beating me. I gasped for air as others fell on top of me. Then the weight started to be lifted; the people on top of me were being dragged away. I heard them screaming for their captors to release them. And then someone lifted me roughly from the ground.

They threw us in a truck, pointing their big guns at us, screaming profanities. I was frightened, thinking about my mom, who had no idea where I was. *What will she do if I die? And Hameed—what is happening to him?* I thought.

It was a hot summer day; we were all soaked with sweat and getting hotter by the second, because we were crammed together with no room to move. Everyone was quiet, afraid to say anything.

19

I could hear my heart beating very fast in my chest and could feel my head pounding and throbbing from the pain. I couldn't stop thinking about air and how there seemed to be none. There was no space between us; it seemed as if we were one big pile of flesh.

The truck stopped, and I heard the sound of a large metal door opening. The truck's door opened, and all we could see were guns pointed at us. Then there was shouting for us to get out of the truck. We walked through the raised metal door and entered the yard, more than ten feet long and surrounded by dark brown and red brick high walls. There were several male guards, dressed in green army uniforms, with short dark hair and thick black beards. Their faces were red, and their eyes bulged as they shouted, "Go, go, go! Move, move!" They led us into a very large and dark room the size of a basketball court. There was only one small window, with vertical black metal bars, very high toward the ceiling. We couldn't see anything outside the window, and no one outside could see what was going on inside that room.

There were many people, some with blood on their clothes or faces, a few of them throwing up, some crying in pain, and the rest staring at the floor quietly, looking pale as death. Without air-conditioning or a fan, the room quickly filled with the foul odor of sweat mixed with vomit and urine. I wanted to throw up. One of the guards shoved me, and I fell. I got up and tucked myself into a far corner. I looked around the room, filled with terror; my body shook uncontrollably, and tears streamed down my face.

My head felt like it was about to explode as the sharp pain at the back of my skull grew. I started hyperventilating. I soon felt the room spinning, and my eyes blurred. I could hear ringing in my ears as I slumped to the floor, unconscious.

CHAPTER 3

Something was hurting my nose. "Ouch," I said in a weak whisper as I felt a sharp pain in my nostrils. I suddenly felt blood running down my face. I opened my eyes and saw a man right in front of my face. I tried to lift my hands or move my body to stop him, but I couldn't; I was very weak. I choked on my sobs because whatever he was doing was clogging my nose. He stopped what he was doing and stared at me.

"Oh, she is alive," he whispered and walked out of the room. As he moved away, I saw he was wearing a white doctor's coat.

I carefully moved my fingers to feel my face; I guessed he had stuck oxygen tubes in my nose.

I was lying in a bed with metal side rails in a white room without windows or pictures. I was covered with white sheets and a brown woolen blanket. There was a dull metal pole to the left side of the bed, an intravenous fluid bag hanging from it with its clear plastic tube running all the way to a vein inside my left arm. There was a large green oxygen tank on the right side of the bed attached to the white plastic tubing that was in my nostrils.

I was scared. I didn't know what had happened or how I had gotten to the hospital—or even what hospital I was in. I wept quietly.

I had been raised Muslim and grew up with a strong faith in God. I was taught that God was love, light, merciful, and kind. I believed that he would answer our prayers, protect us, support us, provide for us, and keep us safe from harm. So, how could it be possible that the new regime was terrorizing and killing people, including innocent young students, in the name of God and Islam? I could not comprehend how cruel they could be, using religious beliefs to get what they wanted.

I don't know how long I lay there with no one looking in on me—it must have been hours—but then the door opened, and my heart soared. My mom and my cousin ran in, tears in their eyes. I had no idea how they had found me, but I was so glad to see them.

"Mom! Is that you? How did you get here? Where am I?"

"Oh, thank God you are alive. We have been searching everywhere for you," said my mom. "You have been in a coma for the past week. We don't know what exactly happened or how you got here."

Together, we learned that I had been in a coma due to a severe head injury. Still, there was a security guard right outside of my hospital room, planning to take me back to jail as soon as I was well enough.

My cousin and her husband were well known in the medical community in Ahvaz. They were able to convince the authorities that I had been at the protest to help injured people, since I was a nursing student. With the grace of God, I was able to get discharged and go to my cousin's home that day and back to Tehran with my mom a few days later. I had no idea what happened to any of my friends or classmates.

I had nightmares every night. I would wake up soaked in sweat from the terror of remembering the gunshots, the blood, the crying, and the sounds of people screaming in pain. I was afraid of going anywhere without my mom, and every little noise made me jump. I was paralyzed by my fears and unable to move forward; I couldn't even take care of myself without help.

"Mom, can you sit here while I take a shower? I am scared. Please don't close the door, Mom!" I would cry in fear.

"I am here, honey. No one could ever hurt you, I promise," she would respond.

My mom was getting exhausted and angry, blaming Hameed for everything that had happened to me. "I raised you right and kept you safe. I taught you how to behave and what to do so you wouldn't be in this situation. Do you have any idea what you have done to me? Can you even imagine how I felt, not knowing if you were dead or alive, or where you had been for a week? Are you going to stop seeing that stupid boy now?"

My family told me that I was very lucky to survive. "They raped and killed many students. They cut their bodies and threw them in the river to die. It's just a miracle that you weren't one of them. We don't know what you were thinking!"

I was paranoid, but I did not regret going to the protest. "I only wanted democracy, freedom of choice and speech, to go to school and have a better life. I wanted to be with my friends and other students to show support and to prove that we need freedom and education. We didn't deserve to be treated that way. I didn't deserve to be tortured that way. No one did," I declared.

I knew it wasn't Hameed's fault, and I refused to let them blame him for the government's violent actions and brutality. He was the only one who could help me heal. He listened to me and understood what I had gone through. Hameed knew why I did it and was proud of me. His love was giving me strength and a reason to live, to try to forget what had happened to me and to be able to move on with my life again. I loved him and couldn't live without him.

I told my mom that I couldn't stop seeing him. "Mom, all my life I obeyed, followed, and listened to everything you said. I can't do it anymore. I love and respect you, but I love Hameed very much. I am so sorry if this is hurting you, but I can't stop loving him."

After a few months, the government decided to close all the universities and colleges. And then one day, I heard on TV about the devastating news of the war between Iran and Iraq.

"Why can't they stop killing people? Why do they need so much blood to be shed for the government to be happy? I just wish we could live in peace," I told my mom.

"It will be over before you know it. I remember many years ago, when you were very young, Iran and Iraq had a quarrel regarding some land, but it was only a few days before it ended," she said, trying to reassure me.

Unfortunately, it didn't stop after a few days. The government officials called all young men to participate in the war. Men who refused were killed if caught; even if they managed to successfully hide, they still faced persecution. Employers were forced to request a certificate to prove the completion of selective services; without it you could not be hired.

"I am not going to kill people," said Hameed.

"What are you going to do? They will kill you if they find out!"

"I don't know. I would rather die than kill innocent people. I am sure I will survive somehow. I have to be careful not to get caught, I guess. Don't worry about me. I will be fine," he said with a smile. "I am going to look for a job. I know I can find one."

"How are you going to find a job when you don't have your certificate?"

"Don't worry. I will find one. There are too many places that hire people and don't care about the stupid government's rules. I promise, I will."

Hameed found a job shortly, working in a small shop as a technician. He was getting paid cash under the table and was very happy to be able to take care of himself. Within a few months, I found a job as a secretary in a company, too. We were both very happy that at least we were able to support ourselves. Hameed was living with his sister and didn't have to pay rent or buy food. It was the same for me; I was living with my mom and family and wasn't expected to pay anything either. It is our culture that adult children live with their parents until they get married.

If my mom couldn't stop us from dating, the government was going to try. The government made a rule that no man should be seen walking next to a woman unless they were related or married.

"I am scared every time we are outside. What if we get caught by security? I have already been to jail. I don't think I will survive another time," I told Hameed.

He looked at me with a smile and said, "Well, I have a great idea. Let's get married then."

"Oh my God, are you serious? How are we going to tell my mom?" I replied.

"I know it's not an easy job, but we have to try. She can't do anything about this. We are old enough to make a decision. We both are working and able to take care of ourselves. I have saved some money, and I can pay for the wedding. I would love to talk to her. I am sure she will agree after she gets to know me!" Hameed exclaimed with excitement.

I was anxious and nervous to tell my mom. We had gone through so much, and I didn't want to rock the boat again. But I had no choice but to find the courage to do so.

"Mom, Hameed asked me to marry him. He wants to talk to you. When do you think he could come over?"

My mom became very angry. "Why, why are you doing this to me? Why do you hate me so much? Do you really want to kill me? Okay, go ahead, just kill me now. I really can't tolerate this anymore!"

"But, Mom, I love him, and I want to marry him. I want to spend the rest of my life with him. I am sick and tired of secrets and want to be able to have a happy life. I am not a child anymore, Mom."

"It is not going to work. You will get divorced. He is too young for you. He can't take care of you, and I know that you will be very unhappy, both of you."

"I am sorry, Mom, but I have made my decision. Please at least give him a chance. Meet and talk with him. That's all I am asking."

"I can't deal with this. I am going to call your aunt. You may not have a father, but she has to hear this. You have to answer to her now. I am going to call her right now."

My aunt came over and played her role.

"Soodabeh, you know that you have a great future ahead of you. There are great men out there, willing and able to take care of you. He is too young, doesn't have an education or a decent job. How is he going to support you? What about school? Are you going to quit school? Oh God, what would you do if your father was here? He would've killed that stupid boy. I know my poor brother wouldn't tolerate this at all," my aunt said.

"No, I am going back to school once the government decides to open them. I can be married and go to school. I love him and can't live without him."

"Are you pregnant? Why don't you understand that he is not good for you? You must be pregnant."

I was in tears. *This is cruel*, I thought. "Why are you accusing and offending me instead of listening to what I am telling you?"

Many hours of screaming, fighting, arguing, and crying passed. My mom lay on the floor in a fetal position, crying. My aunt was angry, pacing the room with her hands in her hair and trying to find the right words or excuses to convince me. It was late in the evening, and everyone was exhausted. When they saw that I wasn't going to change my mind, they finally gave up and decided to make an effort to at least meet Hameed and his family.

I called Hameed to inform him of the great news. "They agreed to meet you and your family. Have you told them yet?"

"Yes, I told them that we are going to get married. They don't agree with us either, but my dad is very supportive. I am sure it would be good for them to meet. You'll love my dad. He is very sweet."

My mom and aunt worked very hard to clean the house and cook food for Hameed and his family. I prayed that everything would work out as we hoped.

Hameed, his mother, his father, two of his sisters, and their husbands came to meet us. I was very shy and sat in a chair quietly, listening to my mom talk.

"I don't think they are smart, thinking that they can get married. They are young and don't have any experience. How do you think they will survive? They don't have decent jobs or an education to support them. What are they going to do when they have kids? Where are they going to live? Do you know how expensive it is to pay rent, buy clothes, and food?" my mom kept ranting.

Hameed's sisters agreed with my mom, but his dad finally interrupted them and said, "I respect your concerns, but I think they are old enough to make a decision and to start living the life they want. I am giving them my blessings and hope the best for them."

After lots of discussions—with Hameed trying to convince them with his charm and plans for our future—they decided to agree with us.

"I would like Hameed and Soodabeh to come and stand by me," said Hameed's father. He then took our hands and put them together and blessed our union.

"I want to wish you many years of happiness, love, and joy. I bless you with God's unconditional and eternal love and light. May you always live in peace and harmony."

My mom and aunt burst into tears, crying—not tears of joy but of sadness. They realized that although they disagreed with our choice to get married, there was nothing they could do except support us. Mom called the rest of our family and told everyone about the wedding. I was very excited that I could talk to Hameed and see him without any fears or worries.

"Have you found a place to live yet?" asked my mom.

"We are planning to go see a place this week."

However, when she found out the area we were thinking about living, she became very upset again.

"You can't live there! That is the worst part of the town."

"But that is the only place we can afford, Mom."

"Yes, that's why I don't want you to get married. You can't afford it. I knew that already, didn't I?"

"I know Mom. I remember what you said. We'll find a place for sure. You don't need to worry about this."

A few days later my mom told me that she had been thinking a lot and decided to let us live upstairs in our house, which had recently been renovated to be its own little apartment, complete with a kitchen.

"Why don't you and Hameed live here until you are able to save money to buy a house?"

I wasn't too excited about that at all. I had planned to move out and live my life without my mom and other family members. Besides, I wasn't sure if Hameed would agree.

"I need to talk to Hameed and will let you know. Thanks Mom."

Hameed was very upset when he heard this. "I can't believe you are even considering this. Don't you know your mother? I don't want to live there. I want to be independent, just the two of us."

"But I don't want to live in the worst area in town. We can't afford to rent a decent place. We have no choice. I hate the idea more than you do, but at least we can save money and buy our house, rather than wasting the money. We are going to have our own place upstairs, not living with them. It's different."

After many discussions, Hameed finally agreed. My mom told us that she would get the house ready for us to move in soon.

"I will take care of everything while you are on your honeymoon," she said.

CHAPTER 4

Hameed was very polite and respectful to my family. He was very kind, gentle, and considerate. He enjoyed interacting with everyone and taking care of my family, especially my youngest brother, Seamak. He was only three years old when my dad died, and Hameed was aware of that. He became a father figure and a great role model for my brother by participating in his school and teaching him everything he needed to know. My mom soon became very supportive of my marriage. She saw how loving and attentive Hameed was.

A few months after we got married, the government reopened some of the colleges and universities. The war with Iraq had injured many soldiers and civilians. They were desperately in need of more doctors and nurses to help the wounded people.

"Did you hear the good news, Soodabeh? There is a nursing program that graduates students as nurses in just one year!" said my mom with excitement.

"Do you think I would get accepted into the program? What if they hear about my past in Ahavaz?"

"No, they won't. I talked to your cousin, and she said that due to the war, all of the documents have been destroyed. They have no proof of your past. You don't have to tell them you were going to nursing school in Ahvaz."

Ahvaz was close to the border between Iran and Iraq. It had been affected much more than other cities, and many places were destroyed as a result of the constant air attacks. I wasn't sure it would be a good idea to lie or hide information from the government, but my mom reassured me that I would be safe.

"I have decided to go back to school, Hameed. I can graduate from the nursing school in one year."

"I think it's a good idea. I agree that you should do this. I am very happy for you, my dear," said Hameed.

I applied for nursing school, and while I was waiting for the result, I found out that I was pregnant. I was so excited to be a mother and start a family, but very disappointed, since I wouldn't be able to go to nursing school. We never talked about getting pregnant and starting a family so soon. I wanted to go to school and become a nurse—to have a career and do what I loved to do. It was very difficult to accept not having the career I had dreamed of. *Maybe God has a different plan for me*, I thought. I decided to tell Hameed right away.

"Oh my God, I am so happy, honey! I can't believe we are going to have a baby so soon!" Hameed said, jumping up and down with excitement.

However, a few weeks later while I was at work, I started bleeding. I called my mom, and she came to pick me up from work. I was so scared and didn't know what to do.

"We should make an appointment with a doctor. I am sure you will be fine," she said.

"You should be on bed rest and off work for a while," said the doctor.

I called my work and notified my manager that I couldn't work until further notice. Resting in bed all the time was making me frustrated. I kept thinking about my life and future. I wanted to be able to attend nursing school rather than stay in bed. School was about to start in a few weeks and I didn't know what to do. I went back to work after a week, since the bleeding had stopped, but after a few days I started bleeding again. Hameed and I were devastated and feeling hopeless.

While at home resting, I heard that I was accepted to the nursing school and could start in two weeks. I was unsure, however, if I could even go to school. *Am I going to lose my baby? Did I do something to deserve this? Am I being punished for thinking about going to school and having a career?* I was confused, stressed, and overwhelmed with fears and guilt.

"Maybe you will feel better by then. Don't worry now. Just make sure to rest and relax. The stress is not good for you," said my mom.

My mom and Hameed thought I should take a chance and go to school. "Well, you don't need to tell them you are pregnant right now. There is no law about getting pregnant while going to school."

I was very happy to have their support, and I decided to go to school. I was scared and prayed that I wouldn't start bleeding again. But the first week of school, while I was standing in the classroom, I felt very dizzy and lost my balance. My friend grabbed me and slowly helped me sit on a chair.

"Are you okay? You look pale as a ghost, Soodabeh. What is going on?"

"I don't know. I think I am getting sick. Could you please call my mom to come and pick me up?"

I started bleeding heavily when I got home. My mom called the doctor and took me there.

"I am sorry, Soodabeh. I think you have lost the baby. We have to send you to the hospital to have a procedure called a D&C to remove any tissue from your uterus lining. We need to be sure there is nothing left inside," said the doctor.

I was in tears and couldn't believe what I had heard. I was tired and needed a break. I hadn't been able to enjoy my life with Hameed yet. We had been married a few short months. Hameed was very disappointed when he found out, but he tried to be brave and supportive.

"Don't worry. We will be fine. Maybe it was meant to be. You are going to school now, and we still have time to have children later. I just want you to be healthy and safe," said Hameed, wiping the tears from my face.

I had surgery the next day. When I opened my eyes, I saw Hameed kissing my face.

"Hey, beautiful. How are you feeling?"

"I am okay, I guess. Have you been here all day? Where is my mom?"

"I sent her home. She was exhausted. Besides, I wanted to be with you alone. I want to take care of you. We don't need your mom to do everything for us," Hameed said with a wink.

"When can I go home?" I asked.

"The doctor said that you can go home tomorrow. I'll stay with you here tonight, and your mom will pick us up tomorrow morning."

Although I was very sad, I knew there must have been a reason I lost my baby. I had to move on with my life and go to school in a few days. My mom made sure that I was taken care of while Hameed was at work.

Life slowly became enjoyable again. All of us were living happily in peace and harmony. Hameed loved his job and was making enough money to support both of us. Mom was ecstatic that I was going to be a nurse.

"I would like us to get pregnant as soon as you finish school," Hameed kept telling me. He bought baby clothes, diapers, and bottles. My family laughed at him when they would see him buying stuff for the baby we didn't have.

"Are you pregnant?" they would ask.

"No. I can't and don't want to get pregnant yet. I need to study, have fun, and enjoy my life first."

"Does Hameed know that you don't want to have a baby yet?" they would ask, laughing at me.

I started the clinical rotation in the hospital and noticed that I liked nursing very much.

"Mom, thanks for encouraging me to go to nursing school. I think I really like it."

"I knew you would. See, Mom is always right," she responded, laughing loudly and proudly.

I finally graduated after a year of hard work and found a job in a university hospital shortly after. As a new graduate, I had to work eighteen-hour shifts every two days, from 2:00 p.m. until 8:00 a.m. the next day. I was exhausted when I got home in the morning, going straight to bed until late in the afternoon. I would get up and start cooking right before Hameed got home. He would also help me, coming to see me at work after his work in the evenings before going home, bringing me food and snacks.

After a few months of working, I found that I was feeling nauseous every morning.

"Hameed, I think I am pregnant."

He grabbed me and started kissing me. "Yes, finally! I am so excited. We have to tell everyone. We need to celebrate!"

When we told our families, everyone was very supportive. But the happiness didn't last long. I started bleeding again. I was so miserable, thinking I would never have any children. *I will never be able to make Hameed happy and give him a child*, I thought.

"Not again," said my mom. "Let's make an appointment to see your doctor, then."

"Sorry, Soodabeh. You know the deal. You have to be on bed rest again," said the doctor.

I called my manager and told her about my situation, crying.

"Don't worry. Just rest and get better," she told me over the phone.

I was bedridden, again, but the bleeding was light and it stopped a few days later. I was happy and back to work, but one week later I was back home on bed rest due to bleeding, yet again. My doctor suggested that I might need to have an easier job so I wouldn't have to lift or do anything strenuous. I called my manager again and informed her of what my doctor had said; she agreed.

"No problem. It happens sometimes with some pregnancies. I am sure we will find something for you to do here. This is a big hospital and there are lots of things you can do. Make sure to take care of yourself, and when ready, you can come back to work," she said.

I was devastated, bored, and depressed. I wanted to be able to keep my baby and be happy again.

Please, God, help me get better. I need to be able to carry my pregnancy to term, I prayed constantly.

I was able to work in a doctor's office during the day, which was much better than working eighteen-hour shifts at the hurried pace of the hospital. I was getting stronger and able to enjoy life, being pregnant and working, doing what I loved to do. Hameed was very happy and would do anything I needed—such as vacuum or clean— and my mom made sure I had everything as well. I felt normal again, looking forward to having my baby soon.

And then two weeks before my due date, right after we ate dinner, something happened.

"Are you okay? Your face is red. What is it?" said Hameed.

"Pain, I have pain ... in my stomach, and ... my back ... uh, it's killing me," I said.

"Do you want me to call your mom?"

"Yes, oh, yes, please. I don't know what's wrong? It's ... uh ... getting ... worse. I can't ... take it ... anymore!" I gasped and ran toward the bathroom as I felt something pushing down all my organs.

"Get out of the bathroom. You are going to deliver your baby there!" my mom screamed. She'd gotten upstairs fast. "You are having contractions," she said, holding my hands and taking me to the living room. "We have to take you to the hospital now. Come on, Hameed, don't you just stand there. Let's take her downstairs. We've got to go!"

The doctor examined me.

"You have had pain and contractions for a few hours but haven't dilated at all. It's not safe for you or the baby. You have to have a C-section right away," he said.

I was terrified when I heard that but also in agony due to the pain. "Please, help me. I can't take this pain any longer!"

The nurse came in the room and got me prepped for surgery. It was past midnight when I was taken to the operating room.

"You are in good hands, Soodabeh. You have the best doctor, and the nurses are amazing," the nurse said with a smile. "When you wake up, you will see your precious baby, I promise." And, I didn't remember anything after that.

I heard a voice asking me, "Are you still in pain, Soodabeh? I just gave you some medicine." I wanted to open my eyes, but I couldn't. "You are done, Soodabeh. You have a beautiful, healthy baby boy. I know you can hear me."

I was able to slowly move my body and open my eyes. I saw Hameed, Mom, my aunt—and, yes, Sara—all by my bedside.

"He is beautiful," Hameed said. "We have a boy. Do you want to see him?"

"Yes, please. I am so happy to hear that. Oh, thank God we finally have a baby."

I wanted to hold him and never let go. He was very small and delicate, under six pounds, with lots of soft black hair and two beautiful black eyes.

"Oh my God, he is a little angel. My baby is so beautiful!" I told Hameed with tears in my eyes—tears of joy.

Hameed's parents and family came to visit one after another, bringing flowers and gifts. Everyone was happy for us. There were hugs, kisses, and laughter in the room. Still, I just wanted to go home and start my life with my husband and our beautiful newborn son, Cyrus. I would be on maternity leave for a few months.

Life was absolutely perfect with my baby. He was the perfect little angel. He slept all night and woke up early in the morning to be fed; then he went back to sleep again for a few more hours. I was on top of the world. Hameed was so excited that he didn't mind changing his diaper or taking care of him, and my mom doted on Cyrus, the first grandchild.

"I just can't wait to come home to see his little face," Hameed would say.

I have the perfect life, I thought. But soon it changed. Hameed's mom became sick, and he had to spend more time with his parents and less time at home.

"What is going on, Hameed?" I asked. "How come you don't like to come home and spend time with Cyrus anymore?"

"You know my mom is sick and needs me. I have to go visit her and make sure she is okay."

Hameed used to call every day from work to talk to me, asking about Cyrus. Although he was exhausted when he would come home, he would play with Cyrus.

I would work, cook, clean, and take care of Cyrus every day. I felt tired most of the time trying to take care of everything. I felt my life had started to fall apart. I loved Hameed very much and wanted to support him, but I felt alone and depressed.

I wanted him to come home and help me, but he had other obligations besides being there for his family. I remembered the time he wanted to have a baby so badly, and I knew how much he loved us and cared for us, but it seemed that I was the one taking care of everything. I felt like a prisoner in my own home.

It was our culture. All women did the same thing. I wasn't the only one taking care of a baby and doing household chores. But I was hoping my life would be different; I had other expectations. I was lost and hopeless but afraid to confide in my family. Mom had warned me about this before.

When I returned to work, I had to take the night shift again. My mom had retired and agreed to take care of Cyrus.

"I can take care of him only if you continue working the night shift. I love and adore Cyrus, and I would do anything to make sure he is safe and taken care of, but I have a life," she requested.

With my busy schedule as a mother and a nurse, I had decided to quit fighting against the government. I had experienced being in prison, had been tortured, and had been in a coma. I wanted to make sure my family was safe. I was done fighting the system. However, Hameed believed in fighting against the government for human rights, democracy, and freedom.

I honored and respected his wish, but I was scared for all of us. I wished he would stop, too. I had no idea what to do, who to talk to, or how to convince him, but I finally decided to discuss the issue with my mom.

"He is out of here. I can't do this anymore. I have welcomed him to my house without paying rent so you can save money, buy a house, and have a better life. What is he thinking? I told you—I knew this would happen!" my mom exploded.

I had no idea what to do or where to go. I felt as helpless as I was about to lose my family and the man I loved. My mom asked me to either leave him or to move out.

CHAPTER 5

We found a house in the neighborhood and moved out of my mom's a few weeks later. My mom and Hameed didn't communicate at all, and I was caught in the middle without any love or support. I had no one to go to and didn't want to create any more friction. So, I decided to find a way to make it work.

My mom agreed to continue taking care of Cyrus while I was working. I would wake up early to cook and clean in order to take Cyrus to my mom's at 1:00 p.m. and go to work right after. I was exhausted most of the time, not being able to rest when I came home from working the night shift. I had to take care of Cyrus.

"You know I don't need your money. I make much more than you. If you don't like it, you can quit your job and stay home with Cyrus. Many women are doing this. So could you," Hameed would say in response to my complaint.

I knew he was right, but I didn't want to. "I don't think so. I am not going to quit my job. I worked so hard to get here, to go to school, and to get a degree to be able to take care of myself. My mom is taking care of Cyrus, and I am going to go to work whether you like it or not," I would say.

Living life that way was depressing and lonely, but my other options were worse. I either had to make it work or crawl back to my mom and live with her. I had dreamed of being independent, married, and raising a family with Hameed. I would cry during the day while at home and would cry myself to sleep most nights.

Hameed tried everything to keep us safe and continued doing what he thought was the best for our family. He never talked about what he did, who was in the antigovernment group, or even where he would go, for the safety of our family. I wasn't allowed to ask any questions at all.

"It's better if you don't know anything. You would be safe if I get caught. No one in the group knows I am married. I would never tell anyone if I get caught either. I want you and Cyrus to be safe," he used to say.

He didn't even wear his wedding band anymore. When my family asked him about this, he offered excuses. "It is very difficult to work with it. I don't want to ruin the ring."

I was trying to change, to be more patient and try not to ask any questions. I would freak out when he was late, not knowing where he was—whether he had gotten caught and was in jail, or if he was just visiting his mom. I had to be the supportive wife, suffer silently, and not say a word in order to keep being married and live with him. I had no idea I was slowly losing my identity, trying so hard to work on our marriage.

My only happiness was Cyrus. He was growing up, the sweetest little baby. His beautiful smile made his little black eyes disappear, and the sound of his laughter was amazing, making my heart melt with love and joy.

I loved my job, too. It was the only place I felt wanted, respected, and honored. Many patients called me their "angel." I would get lost there, forget my pain and loneliness, trying to help others, ease their pain and suffering, and put smiles on their faces. I was satisfied and content when I was at work, knowing that I was doing something right. It was rewarding; it filled my heart with warmth and peace from people who truly needed and appreciated my help and expertise.

The war between Iran and Iraq intensified. It wasn't just the borders that were being targeted and destroyed; the fighting had spread to all the cities. We would hear sirens in the middle of the night and had to turn off all the lights, so fighter pilots couldn't see anything. Then, in a few minutes, if the air strike hit close to us, we would hear a loud noise and feel everything shake as if there were a massive earthquake. When that settled, there would be sirens of police cars and ambulances.

I hated to go to work, because if an attack happened while I was there, I had to deal with not knowing whether my son, husband, or the rest of my family were alive or not. I had to focus on my patients in the unit, making sure they were safe. During raids, I cared for people in the hospital, yet I was unable to take care of my own family. I would run to the phone right after an attack was over to call my mom. And every morning when I got home from work, I would hold and kiss Cyrus. I would cry for those who had lost their family and friends as I watched the news about the night before.

No one was immune any longer. There was always a funeral for someone, either someone who had lost his or her life due to the air attacks or a soldier who had lost his precious life on the battlefield. We had all lost the ability to live a happy life; there were always tears of sadness and despair.

Hameed was communicating better since I had changed and stopped asking questions about where he would go or what he would do. Cyrus was about three years old and had a great relationship with Hameed. They spent time together, laughed, and played when Hameed was at home. He was Daddy's boy. Hameed clearly adored Cyrus. He was able to take him for walks and give me some time and space to rest and relax. Our life was getting better, and he had become more affectionate, kind, loving, and responsible. We were able to communicate, play, and have fun. We could go hiking on the weekend, taking Cyrus with us, and enjoy life as a happy family.

I started thinking of having another child, since we were getting along.

"What? Are you crazy?" Hameed said when I told him. "We are just enjoying our lives. Why do you want to make it complicated again?"

"I know, but I want another baby. We can't have just one child."

"Are you going to complain that you have to take care of another baby?" he said sarcastically.

"Well, you are going to like it, too. Don't you want another cute baby? Maybe this one would be a girl."

"Oh yes, I'd love to have a girl. I know she would be Daddy's girl and love her dad."

"Okay, now you want a girl. What if it's a boy?"

"It better not be. I know I would have a girl. I am 100 percent positive."

We got pregnant after a few months. Hameed was very excited and kept saying that it would be a girl. His family would laugh at him every time he said, "I know we are having a cute baby girl."

"How do you know that? You seem to be very positive," they would ask, making fun of him.

"I don't care what you say. You can laugh as much as you want, but I promise you it will be a girl. I am the father, I created her, and I am sure."

A few weeks later into the pregnancy, I started bleeding, not as bad as the last two times I was pregnant, but enough for the doctor to order bed rest for me again. Hameed tried to help as much as he could since we didn't live with my mom anymore. I got better within a week and went back to work, but I had to work in the office again, so I didn't have to do heavy work such as lifting patients.

I thought I felt better and was back to normal, but I was faced with another challenge—an extreme case of morning sickness, vomiting several times during the day. I was dehydrated and had to have intravenous fluids twice a day. Still, I worked.

One of my coworkers would start intravenous fluids for me, and then I would work. In the evening, another of my friends would start another line. That was my life for over a month, and then I was able to tolerate food again.

I was very happy, not knowing that the feeling wouldn't last that long. I was at the end of the second trimester when Hameed's father got very sick. I was distraught. He was a wonderful, kind, and loving man. He was always polite and respectful of others, a sensitive man who would cry when he saw people injured or dead due to the war, even on TV. He was in his seventies, a retired teacher, and very educated; he spoke several different languages and had written many books about philosophy. I loved and respected him like my own father.

Soon after he was taken to the hospital, I got a phone call from Hameed. "He is not doing well. It seems that his diabetes is out of control, affecting his heart and kidneys. They said that he has to stay there for at least a few days."

"He will be okay soon. He is a strong man, and he will get better. Let me know if I can do anything, please."

Though he had to work during the day, Hameed stayed with him in the hospital every night. I visited him sometimes, but I had to work and take care of Cyrus. He was discharged after a week but was still fatigued.

"I want to stay at my parents' to make sure Dad is okay," said Hameed. "Do you want to go home, or do you want to stay there with me?"

"I want to stay with you. I am a nurse, after all. You may need me. Plus, I want to see you."

I took my blood pressure cuff and stethoscope with me. It was late that first evening when I noticed that Hameed's father looked particularly pale and weak. I checked his blood pressure but could barely hear anything. I checked one more time but felt nothing again. I called Hameed over.

"Dad, are you okay?" Hameed asked him, touching his chest, but he didn't respond.

Hameed looked at me and said, "What should we do?"

"He needs to be taken to the hospital right away. I am not sure what is going on, but he is getting worse."

Hameed went to talk to his family and called for an ambulance to take him to the hospital. Hameed's mom ran into her husband's room screaming and started shaking him.

"Honey, honey, please, honey, open your eyes!" she kept repeating. "Oh my God, what happened? He was talking to me not long ago. He just ate his dinner. Honey, are you okay?"

"Mom, he is going to get better. Please, let them take him to the hospital. Please, don't worry," I said. I tried to calm her down to allow the paramedics to transfer him to the stretcher.

Hameed and his brother-in-law returned from the hospital after a few hours. "What happened? Is he okay?" I asked Hameed.

He took me to his room and started crying quietly. "He is gone. They couldn't do anything for him. It was too late. His internal organs failed, and he died right after we got there."

I held him in my arms, both of us crying. I knew the pain of losing a loved one; I had lost my father many years before. When I married Hameed, I felt as if his dad had become my father, too. Now, it seemed as if I had lost my father all over again. I was grieving for the loss of both of them—my dad and Hameed's father.

"He told me that he would die soon," said Hameed's mom, in tears. He told me right before dinner, but I didn't believe him. What am I going to do without him? I don't want to go on. Please, why, why did you leave me?"

I called my mom the next day and told her that Hameed's dad had died.

"I am on my way. I know how they feel. How are you doing? This is not a good time for you to experience this," said my mom.

My mom was right. The day after the funeral, I woke up with pain in my lower back and abdomen. I was worried I would start bleeding again.

"You've got to go see your doctor. This is not good for you. I knew it," said my mom.

"God, I am sick and tired of this. Why can't I be pregnant like normal people? Why should I constantly suffer with each pregnancy?" I cried to my mom.

We were able to see the doctor as soon as we got to the clinic. "You should be very careful and rest for the next few days," the doctor said. "You are having early contractions. Although they are not severe, there is a chance you could deliver your baby now. This is a critical stage of pregnancy, and the baby would not survive if you delivered early," said the doctor.

"I promise I am going to be careful. I am going to rest, but I have to be with Hameed. He needs me."

I went back to Hameed's parents' home but was very embarrassed that I also had to be cared for. Hameed and his family were very supportive.

"We know that you have to rest. Dad loved you very much. You know that. Of course he wanted you and the baby to be safe and healthy. He was excited when Hameed asked him to name the baby. Please, you go and rest. We understand," said Hameed's mother, crying.

My mom visited every day, knowing that we all needed help and support. Hameed slept in his father's bed every night. He wasn't talking that much, and I could hear him crying quietly when he was alone in the room. He was trying to be strong for his mom and the rest of the family.

Hameed, Cyrus, and I left to go home after a week. But life was not the same. Hameed was depressed, barely talking to me or interacting with Cyrus. I tried to keep our son occupied so he wouldn't bother Hameed. I knew that it would take time for Hameed to get better; he needed to be alone and grieve in his own way. He would go to work during the day and go to see his mom in the evening before coming home. By the time he got home, he was exhausted and had nothing to talk about.

"I know how you feel, Hameed. I have been there. I still miss my dad. But not expressing your feelings is not healthy. Please, at least let me help you."

"I am worried about my mom. She is not eating, sleeping, or taking care of herself, and she's getting weaker every day. I am afraid I will lose her, too."

"I know, honey. I felt the same when my dad died. Every time my mom would leave the house, I would think she was going to die too. This is normal."

"No, you don't understand. Your mom was young, but my mom is old. She doesn't know how to live without my dad."

"Well, do you want to move there and live with her for a while? I have no problem doing that. But, being in so many places and carrying all these burdens alone is not healthy for you either."

"You will do that for me?" asked Hameed.

"Of course. Why not? I love you and your family. I know it won't be easy, but I am willing to do whatever it takes to help."

"Let me think about it first. I need to talk to my mom, too."

A few days later, Hameed told me that his sisters disagreed with us living there, as they were already there, but they did want him to visit her every day.

"That's okay," I said. "I don't mind you going to visit your mom. I just don't want you to get sick. We all need you."

I returned to work. I had occasional pain in my back and abdomen, but it wasn't really bothersome. My doctor told me that as long as I rested when I had pain, I should be okay. I wasn't allowed to hold Cyrus or to lift anything heavy. Life was pretty good again. I had no idea that it wouldn't be long before a storm would shake our foundation to the core.

CHAPTER 6

One night as we finished eating dinner, Hameed looked at me and said, "I need to talk to you about something important." His face was red, and sweat was forming on his forehead. He moved to kneel on the floor in front of me, fidgeting. He reached to hold my hands; his were shaking. He looked into my eyes and continued.

"I'm in great danger. The government is looking for me. They have arrested some of our people, and one of them betrayed the whole group."

As he explained the situation, I felt sick to my stomach. I had been afraid of this moment for so long. Long ago, he had warned me about the possibility of this coming. Just talking about it used to make me frightened, and now I had to face the reality. The thought of losing the love of my life was absolutely unbearable.

"Oh my God, what are we going to do?" I asked. I burst into tears and ran into the bathroom, where I vomited.

Hameed came in and started kissing my head and rubbing my back. "I am sorry, honey. I don't know what to say. I have known this for a while but didn't know how to tell you. I am so sorry. It is the worst time with you being pregnant, but you need to know what is going on before it's too late. I want you to be prepared."

"What do you mean? Prepared for what? How?"

"I have been thinking lately … about escaping to America," said. He rushed on as he saw the color go out of my face for a second time that evening. "But I am worried about leaving you and the kids. I don't even know if I would make it. But I don't know what else to do."

I spoke before I could think. "Yes, please. I want you to go. You should escape. That's the only way. I don't care how much it is going to cost. We will sell everything and get the money. I don't want to raise my kids without a father." I knew why he was thinking of America; his brother, Reza, and his Sister, Maryam, were already living there.

"I talked to Mom, and she said that she could loan me some money to escape," Hameed said. "We are not sure how to do this, but at least we know that I have the money. It may be a long time before you and the kids can join me. Are you sure you are up to this?" Hameed asked.

I knew there were no other options. He had already discussed everything with his family, and they were willing to help him escape. I had to be strong and support him as well, or I would lose my husband forever.

"Yes, this is the only chance we have. We don't have time to think about me or the kids—we will survive. You are the one I am worried about," I responded.

I dreaded telling my family about the nightmare I was facing. I knew that there was only one way for Cyrus and me to stay in Iran—by living with my mother and brothers.

When I told my mom and brother, Soson, they became very upset and angry.

"Have you lost your mind? What if Hameed gets there and forgets all about you and the kids? You should go with him. You love him so much that you can't even think or see clearly!" my mom exploded.

"Mom, I think you are being very irrational. We don't have money for all of us to leave Iran. I am seven months pregnant, and we have a four-year-old child. We don't even know if Hameed can make it out of Iran safely."

My family refused to accept Hameed's leaving without us. "How many times have you begged him not to do this?" Mom asked.

"That's why I was angry. That's why I told you to leave him or move out of my house. That's why I told you not to marry him to begin with."

"I have made my decision, Mom," I said.

I was trying to hide my emotions. We didn't have time for crying; I had to be strong for all of us. I knew there would be enough time to cry, feel sorry for myself, or be lonely and depressed later, after he left.

I had an appointment with my obstetrician for a sonogram. Hameed went along, hoping to learn the gender before he left.

"Sorry, I can't tell," said the doctor.

"That's okay. I am just happy to see and hear the baby's heartbeat," Hameed responded with a smile, looking at the doctor.

After we left the doctor's office, Hameed looked at me and said, "I was talking to my dad when he was sick in the hospital. I asked him what to name our baby if it was a girl."

"What did he say?"

"Azeeta."

"Oh, I love that name," I told him, smiling.

We tried to enjoy every minute together, continuing to plan our future.

But there were times I could see the pain in Hameed's eyes. He would grow quiet, lost deep in his thoughts, staring at the floor or the wall. I would leave the room, pretending that I had to go to the bathroom, crying silently. I didn't want him to see any signs of weakness; I was afraid he would change his mind. I knew how painful that must have been for him—leaving us behind, not even knowing what the future would hold.

"I don't know what to do for you. How can I ever thank you for staying here with your mom and family so I can leave? I am forever grateful to have you in my life. I will take care of you and the kids again—I promise. We will have a better life in America," Hameed said.

I called my mom and told her that Hameed would be leaving soon, but she hung up the phone as soon as she heard that. I was in pain yet had no one to support or comfort me. I wished my mom would understand that I had no choice but saving Hameed's life. He was my husband and the father of my children. I had lost my father and knew how it felt to grow up without one. I saw how hard my mom had to work to take care of us. I witnessed all the sacrifices she had made for us. I knew that at least I had hope that—maybe with the grace of God—Hameed would make it to America and spare my children and me a repeat of the life I had already led.

The war between Iran and Iraq had been going on for eight years, but it ended the day before Hameed left.

"See, this is a good omen, Soodabeh. At least I won't worry about the war," Hameed said, smiling.

I will never forget the day he left. Hameed held me in his arms, tightly, and neither one of us was able to let go. I could hear the sounds of his heart beating fast. I couldn't stop crying.

"You know I never say good-bye," Hameed said, looking in my eyes.

"I know. Since I met you, you have never said that."

"So, what should we say?"

"See you later, my love."

"Yes, that's right. I'll see you soon." He hugged me again, kissing my forehead.

"Cyrus, come on, baby. Say good-bye to Dad," Hameed said, looking at Cyrus.

"Dad, when are you coming back?"

"Soon, buddy, soon. You are going to be a good boy, okay? Listen to Mom and Grandma. I am counting on you, baby. Love you so much," Hameed said, while hugging and kissing Cyrus.

He left. The man I loved left me, and I had no idea if I would ever see him again. He left, walking down the alley toward the main street where we used to live and never looked back. I stood there, holding Cyrus's hand, watching until he disappeared. I felt really sick. I took Cyrus inside, ran to the bathroom, and started vomiting.

I washed my mouth and face and went to the bedroom, closing the door behind me so Cyrus couldn't see or hear me. I was there, alone, on my knees, crying and praying. *Oh, dear God, I can't live without him. God, you know that I have no one to count on but you. Please, God, take care of my baby. Just keep him safe. Please, God, I beg you, please.*

Mom and Soson came and took us to Mom's house. I wanted to be left alone and not interact with anyone, ever again. My heart was aching in pain. Tears ran down my face as I looked out the window, trying to hide my face. I heard Soson trying to answer Cyrus's questions about the reason his dad had left and when he was coming back. My mother was silent the whole way home, too—but she was quiet because she was giving me the silent treatment.

CHAPTER 7

I had been working as a nurse at the university medical center for over five years when Hameed left. Although I had lots of friends there, I was unable to tell anyone that my husband had escaped the country. I was in pain, yet nobody knew. I would put on a fake smile and go to work every day. The love I had for my job gave me the strength to take care of my patients. In turn, they loved and respected me, which left me feeling happy, satisfied, and actually eager to go to work every day.

A few weeks passed before I heard from Hameed. "Hi, Soodabeh. How are you doing?" I burst into tears of excitement when I heard his voice.

"Oh my God, it's so good to hear your voice! Where are you?"

"I am in Turkey, doing really well. How is Cyrus? I miss you guys so much. How is the baby? Please tell her I love her so much," Hameed answered. "May I talk to Cyrus, please?

I was so happy to know he was safe. I wanted to ask him how he got there and know the details of his journey. But I knew he couldn't tell me anything about it. I started selling everything we had, from jewelry to the bedroom set to dishes and clothes—everything. Selling my belongings was very hard for me; I was selling things that were part of my life. But I knew that I had no other choice. I kept thinking about the wonderful life I would have with my family in America.

Hameed was staying with his nephew in Ankara, Turkey, so he had a stable address. I was happy to be able to write him letters or call him. He had to stay in Turkey for a while, waiting to receive money from his brother, Reza, to get a passport.

I received letters from Hameed every week, promising the wonderful life we would have together. "I love you, Soodabeh, very much, more than you have ever known. I can't imagine life without you. I am proud of you and very grateful for what you have done for me. I know you are having a tough time there, but I promise I will take care of you and our family. You will see. I will show you, baby, I promise—soon."

He wrote poems, confessing his love and devotion to me. It was unusual for Hameed to ever say "I love you" when we were living together. Although it was unlike him to say so before, it seemed that he had found a way to express his feelings. His poems and love letters made me extremely happy and hopeful. They gave me the strength to be able to move on, and a reason to live.

I was getting bigger and was ready to deliver the baby soon. I went to see my doctor a few weeks before my due date. "You have a choice to wait and see if you can deliver your baby naturally or to have a C- section, since you already had one with your first baby," my doctor told me.

"No, I can't tolerate the pain for many hours only to find out that I have to have a C- section anyway. Could we go ahead and schedule it for next week, on June 18th, please?" It was one week before my due date, but I chose that day because it was my wedding anniversary. My doctor accepted without any objections.

I was nervous and couldn't sleep the night before the surgery. I kept thinking about Hameed, the way he had been there for me when I had to go to hospital to deliver Cyrus. The birth of my second child should have been a happy occasion, but not having Hameed with me, I felt all alone and depressed. *Please, God, help me, please,* I prayed. *I don't know how to go on any longer. I have no strength in me at all. How am I going to take care of another child?* Then I cried myself to sleep.

I woke up the next day, the day I had to check into the hospital, feeling anxious and scared. I was looking forward to holding my baby in my arms, yet I was nervous to take care of her all alone, without Hameed. My mom wasn't happy about me being pregnant, anyway.

"Why did you get pregnant again? He knew that there would always be a danger. Why did he decide to have another child then?" she kept asking me. Mom knew that she had to deal with another baby, working harder to take care of us. I felt as if the happiest moment of my life had turned into a very dark and depressing one.

I was lost in my thoughts when I heard my mom's voice. "Soodabeh, I am going shopping, taking Arman with me."

It was the day before my scheduled C-section. *How could it even be possible that she doesn't remember I had to go to the hospital? She doesn't even care to ask me how I am feeling these days,* I thought. *I wish she would. I wish she knew that I am scared and lonely. How can she be this way? I am sure I won't do that to my children.*

As soon as she left the house, I packed my clothes in a small bag and took a bus to the hospital. I tried not to cry on the bus, as I didn't want anyone to notice me. I tried to focus on the love Hameed had for me, the amazing life he had promised would be waiting for me, and the beautiful little angel I was about to give birth to.

I signed myself into the unit and went to my room, tears running down my face like a river. *How did I end up here? I am so lonely, God. I miss my husband, the love of my life. Please, God, at least keep him safe,* I prayed before going to sleep.

The nurse woke me up early in the morning. "Hey, Soodabeh, are you ready?" she asked.

"Yes, I am. I can't wait to see my baby. I am ready!"

"Where is your husband?"

"He had to stay home with Cyrus. He will come and visit me later," I lied to the nurse, my heart aching with pain.

"Okay, don't worry. We are here to do the best we can. You know you'll be okay, right? By the time you wake up, you will see the little angel. Do you know if it's a boy or a girl?"

"No, I don't. We had an ultrasound, but the doctor couldn't say for sure. I wish I knew. I want to have a little girl, but I would settle for a healthy baby, of course."

I woke up to the sound of one of my coworkers, Sara, calling my name. "Soodabeh, it is a girl." I could barely keep my eyes open, but I could hear her well.

Oh my God. Hameed was right. We have a baby girl, I thought. All my pain vanished the minute I heard Sara's voice.

I opened my eyes and saw Sara standing by my bedside, smiling. "It is about time you wake up, my dear. How are you feeling? Do you want to see her? She is very small but really beautiful."

"Yes, I do, Sara. Can you bring her now?" She nodded and left the room.

A few minutes later, Sara came back with my daughter and put her in my arms. I noticed her pinkish white skin, her fine light brown hair, and her little angelic face, looking at me with her dark black eyes, making my heart melt with joy. She was small and delicate, under six pounds, the same size Cyrus had been when he was born.

"Oh my, I am so glad to finally see you, sweetheart. Mommy loves you very much. Welcome to our family, sweetie." I couldn't stop looking at her, wishing that Hameed was there to see her. He got what he wanted—to have a daughter—but was unable to hold or even see her.

I gave thanks to God, and I named her Azeeta, as was chosen for her by her grandfather, Hameed's dad.

I was discharged a few days later. I called Hameed the first night I got home. "It is a girl, Hameed. You were right, honey. We have Azeeta, born on our wedding anniversary. Isn't it awesome?" I told Hameed over the phone.

"Are you serious? Wow, this is amazing. I am so proud of you, baby. I wish I could be there to see you guys," he said. I could hear him crying over the phone.

"Well, hopefully we will see you soon. I miss and love you, Hameed."

"Me too. Please take care of yourself. Make sure to tell her that Daddy loves her very much and can't wait to see her."

I was sad, thinking about how Hameed must be feeling, unable to see or hold his daughter. I remembered how excited he had been when Cyrus was born. Thinking of the good memories we had, celebrating the birth of our first child, made me miss him even more. I had many family members coming to visit, including Hameed's family, but nothing took his place. Nothing was the same anymore. I wanted my husband to be there to share this beautiful moment with me.

I started thinking about the uncertain future as I was lying in bed every day. With the new baby, my mom had to work harder taking care of all of us. My mom took care of Azeeta, since I had had a C-section and was unable to do so for a while. She didn't show any emotions, except to complain that she was tired all the time. We communicated only when I needed something or if she had questions about Cyrus or Azeeta.

Watching my little baby girl grow filled my life with joy and happiness. I had a reason to get up in the morning, looking forward to taking care of my children. Cyrus, however, was missing his father more and more every day. He would burst into tears without warning, but especially before bed. It was heart wrenching for me to see him suffer, not being able to ease his pain.

Hameed and I kept in contact by phone and letters mostly, saving expensive phone calls for only the most important news. One night he called me with the biggest news yet.

"Soodabeh, I am going to leave in a few days. The next time I call you, I will be in America."

"Oh, thank God. Finally! I am so glad to hear that. I can't wait to see you soon. Have a safe trip, baby. I love you so much."

I expected to hear from Hameed in a week, but heard nothing for a few weeks. I kept asking Hameed's family if they had heard anything from Reza or Maryam, but they would tell me that they didn't know anything either. I was worried sick, but I knew that the only thing I could do was to pray. Weeks turned into months. I was hopeless and miserable.

"I am sure he got there and forgot all about you and the kids. That's all he needed. I knew that," I would hear from my mom and the rest of my family. I couldn't believe how cruel they could be, hurting me with their comments.

"I know he wouldn't do that to me. I trust him 100 percent. I know he would have called if he could," I would respond, in tears with a broken heart.

One night, while I was watching TV, I heard the phone ring. "Hi Soodabeh, it's me. I am at Reza's house in America. How are you guys doing? How are Cyrus and Azeeta?"

"Oh, goodness! I'm so glad to hear your voice again!" I said. I was crying so hard I could barely breathe. "I am glad you are alive. Where have you been?"

"I am okay now. You don't have to worry about me. I am here and alive. I miss you guys so much. Please send me some pictures of the kids."

I knew that Hameed was unable to tell me how he got there or what had happened for the past few months. It wouldn't be safe for us to talk about it over the phone. I was just so grateful he was alive and well. And I knew I didn't have to answer to the accusations of him forgetting about the kids and me any longer.

I went to see Hameed's family to celebrate that he had made it to America. However, it was then when I found out that his family had known where Hameed had been all along.

"I am sorry we couldn't tell you that he got arrested the first time he was planning to go to America. He was in jail for a while, waiting for more money to get out of there. So, when he got out of jail, we thought it would be best if you didn't have any contact with him until he arrived there. We were trying to protect him," his mother told me.

I just sat there, my body frozen cold, unable to do or say anything. I was wondering how they could let me be miserable and not know anything about Hameed. But I was happy that he was safe. I couldn't wait to finally join him and start a new life.

I was grateful for the fact that Hameed was alive and had made it to America. I was very excited thinking that I would be able to see him very soon. Hameed called me a few weeks later and said,

"I had to get a lawyer to help me with my permanent residency. I am not sure how long it may take, but I am very hopeful. Just hang in there, honey. It's going to happen soon, I promise." Hameed had to get his permanent residency in order to be able to apply for us to come to America.

But after a year, my children and I were still living with Mom and two of my brothers. My brothers were sharing one of the bedrooms, I had the other one with the kids, and my mom was sleeping in the living room. Cyrus's running around and Azeeta's crying kept my family awake most nights.

"I don't know what Hameed is doing there," Mom said. "How come you are still here taking care of his kids? What happened to all the promises he had given you? When are you going to leave? Isn't it time yet?"

I was exhausted and irritated too. I worked six days a week and took Cyrus and Azeeta to daycare every morning before going to work. I was unable to afford a car, so I had to take two buses to go to work every day. I would get up early in the morning, get Cyrus and Azeeta ready for daycare—which was a nightmare—and then I would be holding Azeeta in my arms, a big bag of their clothes, diapers, and food on my shoulders, and holding Cyrus's hand trying to catch a bus.

I decided to work extra days, which meant I worked fifteen days in a row, had one day off, and went back to work for the next fifteen days. I only had two days off every month. I thought that was the best way to stay out of the house, allowing my family to have some peace and quiet, while I was at work and my kids were in day care.

I was miserable, working hard, taking care of the kids, and answering the big question of why I wasn't able to go to America to join Hameed.

"I knew that would happen. I told you so. He probably found someone else. Why should he wait so long otherwise? There are many people that had gone to America in less than a year. What is he doing there?" Eventually, Mom decided not to help me with the kids at all.

"I am tired of doing everything, taking care of everyone, cooking and cleaning every day. You need to push Hameed and ask him to do something. He won't do anything if you don't ask, Soodabeh."

The fighting and arguing continued every day. It was to the point that I would just listen and not say anything at all. I had no strength in me to argue any longer. I was praying that God would help me wake up every day to go to work and take care of my kids.

I woke up to go to work one day, and suddenly I felt dizzy and nauseated. I ran to the bathroom, vomiting. My mother was sleeping and didn't even notice. I washed my face and mouth, took Cyrus and Azeeta, and left the house.

By the time I got to work, I felt really sick and my body was very hot, like an oven. "Wow, Soodabeh, are you okay?" my supervisor asked me.

"No, I don't think so. I threw up before leaving the house, and I think I have a fever."

"Go see the doctor at urgent care right away. You can't work like this."

I walked to the urgent care since it was right next door. "You have to be admitted. Not sure what is going on, but we have to keep you under observation."

"Farah, could you call my sister-in-law to pick up the kids, please?" I asked one of my coworkers. I knew that my family would not be supportive or wanting to take care of my kids, but I was sure that Hameed's older sister would, since she loved them so much. I trusted her to take care of the kids while I was in the hospital.

I had to stay there for ten days, running a high fever the whole time, and they were unable to find out the cause, in spite of all the tests. I had several different intravenous antibiotics, but none were effective, leaving the doctors wondering how to save my life. Cold sores spread all over my mouth, inside my nostrils, and all the way down my throat—to the point where I couldn't eat or even drink; I was alive with intravenous fluids only. My arms were black and blue from the needles. I was very depressed, crying all the time, and wishing that my husband were with me.

One night when I was laying on the hospital bed, I had a dream. There was a woman, very tall—as if she could touch the ceiling—in a white and sheer long dress, with long blond hair. I could see the light emanating from her pores as she looked at me, smiling.

"Fear not," she said with a gentle voice, trying to comfort me. "Everything will be all right. You have nothing to worry about, my child," she said before she disappeared.

I woke up, trying to make sense of the dream. "Wow, she was so beautiful," I said aloud, still remembering the intense light I had seen. *Could that have been an angel?* I thought. Even thinking about it was making my heart filled with an unconditional love, leaving me feeling exceptionally peaceful.

I had never seen anything like that before. Although I had heard of angels, I had never thought about them; nor did I know what they looked like. I was taught that angels were messengers of God, only visible to saints and prophets. *No, it must have been a dream. I am not worthy of seeing an angel, I know. But it was such a magnificent dream,* I thought.

I woke up with the sound of the nurses calling my name. I opened my eyes and saw Farah, trying to wake me up to check my temperature.

"Wow, Soodabeh, finally, no fever!" Farah told me with excitement.

"Are you serious?"

"Yes, do you want to see?"

"Oh, God, thank you. I hope I can get better and go home. I miss my kids so much," I said. I was very excited to be able to get discharged from the hospital and to see my children again. I was discharged the next day. When I went home, I told my mom about the dream I had.

"I am so glad. That means that your problems will be over soon. Maybe you will hear from Hameed soon to let you know that it's time for you guys to join him."

My family felt sorry for me at first, but after one week, life became the same again. I had to go back to work every day and take care of the kids. I was hopeless and depressed. I prayed to be able to hear from Hameed soon.

One day, he finally called. "I have my permanent residency and I'm finally able to apply for you guys to join me, but I don't know how long it would take."

"I am sick and tired of waiting, Hameed. I don't think you have any idea what I am going through at all."

"Please don't push me. I am trying to save some money and get an apartment so that when you come here, you will be comfortable. I have no control over the government. We have no choice but to wait. I am miserable, too. I miss my family, the baby I haven't even seen. Do you really think it's a picnic for me here? It is going to take time, and no one knows how long."

I was exhausted listening to my family complaining and Hameed telling me to wait longer. I wish I knew how long I had to wait; maybe it would have been easier. But at least I was sure that Hameed loved me and wanted the kids and me to have a better life. We were still communicating by weekly letters and monthly phone calls, and I wasn't the only one Hameed was making promises to.

"Cyrus, I will see you soon, buddy," I would hear him say, a huge smile growing across our son's face. "Take care of your little sister and Mom, okay? I love and miss you so much, baby."

He wouldn't lie to a child, would he? I remembered my father when he worked for the agriculture department. His job required him to spend a lot of time away from home in remote areas in the country, opening department offices and serving as an advocate for the farmers and low-income families. When he called home, my mom would express how difficult it was for her to raise us kids alone—as she felt she was doing so much of the time—and I would cry and cry, begging him to come home. He would promise he would as soon as he could, and he would say that he loved me.

Hameed is right—I have to be patient, I thought. I believed and trusted him with all my heart, knowing that he would do anything and everything to help us to reunite again.

I took Cyrus and Azeeta to a photographer and sent the pictures to Hameed. He gushed over them during our next thirty-minute phone call, and for a minute I could imagine that we were in the same room again, that I could see him, touch him, and kiss him.

But my next letter was not met with a reply for quite a long while. Eventually, the letters stopped completely. I was concerned, thinking maybe he was sick. So I called him earlier than scheduled.

"I have so much to do and no time to sit down and write to anyone," he responded. "I am going to work and school. By the time I do my homework, I barely have time or energy to write."

"I am sorry that you have to work so hard, but your letters are the only hope I have. You know I have no one to talk to. I can't talk to my friends or family. I am feeling lonely here, Hameed."

"I am sorry. I am only one person, and I can't do everything. I haven't even written to my mom or family. I just don't have any time," he said. I said no more.

The next time I went to visit Hameed's family, his mother greeted me angrily. She was not getting any letters from Hameed either, and she blamed me. "I know he is working so hard to take you guys over there. My baby must be exhausted not to have any time to write to us."

"I am sorry, Mom, but I don't see that as an excuse. I am busy, too, raising two small children and working every day." I was tired of being the scapegoat, being blamed for everything Hameed had done. I was suffering day and night, caught between my family and his, trying to defend him nonstop. It had been a nightmare for two years, and I wanted it to be over soon.

Living in a cramped apartment in a bustling city, I felt a deep loneliness engulf me. It was making me feeling lonely and depressed, more than I ever thought possible. I was my own person, with a degree and a career, and I had proved I could take care of myself and my children, but going at life alone was not what I wanted. *No*, I realized. *That's not what I wanted.* If I hadn't met Hameed, I wouldn't have two young people depending on me, I wouldn't have a family of in-laws making demands of me, and I would likely already be in America, having long ago gone there for school. The thought of losing Hameed was unbearable, because I would be left alone dealing with the life he had created for me.

One night I had a dream that Hameed was with another woman; she was tall with red hair and was very beautiful. They were walking, hand in hand, talking and laughing. I woke up soaked in a cold sweat, my mouth dry, my body shaking, and my heart racing so fast, remembering the horrible dream.

I was exhausted and crying in my room when I got home. Soson, ever kind, heard my cries and sat with me, listening to me blubber about my fears. After thinking a moment— his palm tracing warm circles on my back—he said, "Well, maybe I can take you and the kids to the American embassy in Turkey. Maybe they will feel sorry for you and give you the visa to go there once they see your situation and hear your story. You are right, Soodabeh. You can't just stay here waiting for Hameed."

"What about Seema and Ali?"

"They'll stay with her mom. Let's plan to go to Turkey as soon as we can, before Seema delivers the baby."

"Oh God, I am feeling guilty now. Are you sure she would be okay with that?"

"Yes, I know she would do anything to help you. We have been thinking about it for a while." He leaned in with a smile, a conspiratorial brother smile. "We have been thinking of your move to America as paving the way for us, anyway. Once you settle in, we'd see if we could join you. So it's very much in our interest to help you."

"Oh my God, Soson. That would be awesome. Thank you so much for doing this. I don't know what to say."

"Call Hameed and tell him that I am going to take you guys to Turkey. He needs to send all the documents he has to help us."

I reached Hameed right away. He agreed to mail the documents. Even though I knew they wouldn't be in the mailbox the next day, I started checking immediately. Once a week had passed, my brain joined my heart. Each time my feet scurried over the driveway's warm cement, I was certain that I'd find the papers in the mailbox. However, after a month, I had to call Hameed.

"I haven't received anything in the mail yet. We are only waiting for you. Seema is pregnant, and Soson needs to take us to Turkey before she delivers the baby," I told him over the phone.

"I don't know. I have already mailed the documents. Just be patient," he said.

I had no idea what was going on. With immigration in sight, though, I almost didn't care. His children needed a father, and I needed to get out of my dead-end situation in Iran. I prayed to God day and night. Walking from one patient's room to another, I'd pray. Changing out of my uniform, I was thinking about traveling and talking to God about it. Every night before I fell asleep, when I heard the quiet breaths of my children and the squawks of the city out my window, I prayed some more.

Of course, life is never just about you; bigger things are always happening. Even if the documents had arrived, I would have been delayed, because two tragedies—one on a family level and one on a national one—happened then.

As I arrived home from work, I heard my mom's voice. "Oh my God, no … no … no. How did it happen?" she said.

I dropped my bag and gathered Azeeta, who had toddled over to see me, in my arms and hurried to Mom.

"Seema's father passed away this morning. He was trying to change the lightbulb in the kitchen when he fell down and hit his head on the ground. They took him to the hospital immediately, but he died on the way to the hospital. They believe that he had a stroke before falling down the leader."

"Oh no …" I couldn't believe it. He was such a wonderful man, only in his early fifties. He had never made a bad comment about anyone and was always kind, caring, and generous. We all loved and respected him very much.

"Soson is on his way to pick me up. Oh God, I have to go. Can you take care of your brothers while I am gone?"

I take that back; in Iran, if you are a male, life is never bigger than you. You remain the top consideration. "Come on, Mom. They are not kids anymore. Don't worry, I will make sure they know what happened. But do you want me to go?"

"No, I don't want to take the kids with us. It's a long drive. I will call you when we get there."

We were still grieving our private loss when a public one happened. It was my day off. I was sitting in the living room reading a book, and Cyrus was playing with Azeeta in the bedroom when everything around me started to shake.

"Oh God, it's an earthquake!" my mom screamed.

Azeeta and Cyrus ran out of the bedroom, crying and pale, their little bodies trembling with fear.

"It's okay, babies, come here. It's an earthquake, honey, but see, it's gone. As quickly as the rumbling had started, it stopped. "I am here. Mom is here, babies," I continued holding them in my arms.

"Turn on the TV," I heard my mom asking me.

"There has been a massive earthquake in the north," said the reporter. "It has destroyed many homes and taken many lives. This is absolutely a tragedy," he continued.

The epicenter was about three hundred miles north of Tehran, yet we could still feel the impact. I couldn't believe my eyes, watching the news.

"No one has ever seen or experienced such massive destruction," the reporter said. "It is as if the earth opened up suddenly and swallowed the cities, houses, and the people living in them. We are unable to distinguish where each city was located."

The news report showed men and women, streaked with dirt and blood; they were wailing and clawing through rubble. I asked my children to go back to the bedroom, but I couldn't look away.

"I don't know why there are so many disasters. We had so much to deal with because of the war, and now the earthquake. I wish we could have some peace here," I told my mom.

"I know. It's one thing after another. I'm wondering what else could go wrong next," my mom responded, wiping her tears.

"Oh, please, don't ask for more. We have enough already."

"No, I am not asking for more. We have enough, God knows, we have," she responded.

These events spurred Soson to take action. Before, we were just trying to go to Turkey before his child's birth; now, we were keenly aware of how fragile everything was. But one of the big reasons we really needed that paperwork from Hameed was because without his signature, Azeeta couldn't travel at all. I had a passport for Cyrus, but a married woman needed her husband's written permission for her to travel with each of her children.

"Don't worry, I will take care of it. Just give me the passport," Soson said.

He came back the next day with a fully prepared passport. "Here, I got it. If I could get my hands on your ... husband," he said shaking his head and laughing.

"How did you do that?"

"I have a friend who's a notary. I took Hameed's birth certificate with me and signed the paper for him. Of course, I gave him money, you know."

"The next time you see me, I'll have my passport, and we'll go!" And he closed the door behind him.

CHAPTER 8

I dreaded going back to work, knowing that every time I took care of a patient, I would think of my brother, remembering I wasn't there to help him, comfort him, or take his pain away. I was wondering what he was feeling or even thinking after the accident. And I wondered how I could help the people he left behind, especially his young children.

Soson's death called to mind my father's death of a sudden heart attack at age forty- seven. I was the oldest of four, with three younger brothers. At that time, I was thirteen; Soson, eleven; Soheil, six; and Seamak, only two years old. My parents had adopted a girl my age named Maggy when her parents died in an earthquake. I knew the pain of growing up without a father, and now I had to witness Soson's children experiencing the same.

My father was a wonderful, kind, and loving man. He always tried to talk gently to us kids. Although he didn't even graduate from high school, he was very intelligent and loved reading books about everything and anything—history, geography, psychology, philosophy, and even religion. In the local café, he and college students talked about what he had learned and read, and he would sometimes help the students with their assignments.

At home, I remember him sitting on the floor, a small table full of books in front of him and many more volumes all around him on the carpet. If the book he was reading referenced a second book,

Dad would buy the other book to read it too. My father was easily able to quote from every book he had read.

"What are you reading, Dad?" I would ask.

"Oh hey honey, come sit by me, and I will show you. Try to see if you can read this sentence for me, baby."

His eyes shone with joy and excitement as he would watch me read. "Do you understand what they are talking about?" he asked.

"Not really, Dad," I responded, laughing.

"Well, it means …" and he would explain in detail.

My father didn't complete high school, because he too lost his father at a young age. My grandfather died when my dad was only sixteen years old, leaving my grandmother with two young children. My grandparents had had many children, but they all had died, except two—my dad and his younger sister. My grandmother was unable to work. Consequently, my father had to quit school and go to work to support his family. He loved and adored his mother and sister and would do anything they wanted. It was in his nature to help and please others.

Unfortunately, he loved eating good food, and a lot of it— sometimes two dinners in one day, one out before coming home from work and one with us—and he hated going to the doctor or taking medications. As a result, his health was poor. He had high blood pressure and heart disease, but no one was aware of it at the time.

We were visiting my grandmother and aunt in Tehran over summer break when Dad got sick. My aunt called an ambulance when she noticed that my father was having difficulty breathing.

"I am not going to let you put me on the stretcher," my dad told the paramedics. "You are scaring my children." He walked outside to be taken to the hospital. Even when he was sick, he was thinking of us, trying to protect our feelings. Still, I was scared.

I was playing with my brothers when I heard the sirens and a loud knock on the door. Although I wasn't quite sure what was going on, I knew intuitively that I was about to face the greatest pain of my life. I walked away from my brothers, hid in a corner, covered my face, and cried.

Soson had a hard time dealing with the death of our father. I was shy and quiet, crying when no one was watching, but Soson was unable to calm down. He would cry from the time we got in the car to go visit our dad's grave until we got there.

"Why, Dad? Why did you leave me here? I don't want to live anymore without you. Please take me," Soson would say over and over. In my memory, it was heartbreaking that an eleven-year-old child suffered so much.

Soson had cared for my children for the past three years. One day, Azeeta called him "Dad." My baby girl didn't know her father and thought Soson was her father. His face became red, and with tears in his eyes he got up and held her in his arms.

"No, I am not your dad, Azeeta. I am your uncle." He knew how she felt.

Late one evening as I was getting the kids ready for bed, I heard the phone ringing.

"Hi, Soodabeh. How are you doing?"

I started crying as soon as I heard Hameed's voice, unable to catch my breath or say any words.

"Soodabeh, please calm down. I need you to listen to me very carefully. I am going to send all the immigration paperwork to the American embassy in Turkey."

"It's too late, Hameed. Now that Soson is gone, you are sending me the papers? Where have you been? Why didn't you do it sooner?"

"Soodabeh, please, just listen. I know you are hurt and angry. But you have got to be quiet and listen just a few minutes, please. I have good news, I promise. When I was in Turkey, I met a very nice young man who became one of my roommates, Ali. I called him to see if there would be any way he might be able to help you. He graciously said you and the kids could stay in his apartment until you get the visa. He promised to take you to the embassy and do whatever it takes to make sure you are comfortable and safe there."

I didn't know what to say. Should I be happy that I was finally getting out of there or sad for leaving my brother's family alone to deal with the pain and heartache of losing him?

I started crying again. "How could I? I just buried my brother last month."

"Please, Soodabeh, this is your chance. I know Soson would have been happy for you."

"Staying here is not going to bring him back, you know," my aunt told me. "You have to go there and maybe try to help his family. You have suffered enough, Soodabeh. You can't solve everyone's problem by staying here, you know."

I decided to buy the plane tickets to Turkey. I had never traveled alone, not even to another city in Iran. I always had someone to take care of me. I was totally dependent on my family and didn't know how to survive without them. Before I got married, my mother did everything for me, and after that, it was my husband's responsibility. The past three years, I had started learning to be more independent, but this would be a true break from my family.

I wasn't happy or excited but sad and guilty. My mother was not talking to me, crying nonstop, grieving for the loss of her son and now us. It had become real for her, suddenly, that we were leaving, and that she may never see us again.

The night of my flight to Turkey our house was filled with family. We were all sad and in tears.

Finally, my aunt guided me to the bedroom away from the rest of the family. "Come on, Soodabeh, you got to focus. Do you have your passport and all the documents you need?"

"Yes, I have them right here, inside my purse."

"How about the things you need for the kids—diapers, baby food?"

"Yes, I have everything." I reached to hug her, having never really stopped crying. "I am scared. What if I won't be able to get a visa? What am I going to do?"

"You don't have time to think about this now, Soodabeh. Get yourself together, baby. Come on, we've got to leave before you miss your flight."

No one said anything in the car to the airport; we just cried. Once at the gate, my mom grasped me and said, "I may never see you again, honey. Please forgive me if I die."

They announced my flight, and I needed to leave, but my feet were stuck to the floor. Finally, one of my cousins helped, starting the kids off, getting me to follow.

I could hear my family crying louder, but I didn't have the heart to look back.

Good bye, Soson. I wish you were here with me. How could I leave without you? I am sorry, baby. I am so sorry. I am the worst sister, I know, leaving your family all alone, at the worst time of their lives. I really wished it was a better circumstance. I wish you were here.

CHAPTER 9

As soon as the kids and I were settled on the plane and there really was no turning back, I transformed from sad to nervous. *What will it be like to live with Ali, a man I've never met? What if he doesn't meet us at the airport? What would I do then? I can't speak the language. With two young children, where would I go?*

We got our two large suitcases: one filled with our clothes and belongings, and the other one filled with food, such as rice, nuts, pastries, dried herbs, and vegetables. I knew that I couldn't afford to buy food in Turkey. I had to save money for our tickets to America.

Holding Azeeta in one arm, dragging two huge suitcases with the other, and making sure that Cyrus was sticking close by me, I finally heard a warm voice calling my name.

"Soodabeh? Soodabeh! Hi, I am Ali!"

"Nice to meet you, Ali! Thank you so much for picking us up." I was thrilled to see him.

"Oh, boy, Cyrus, you look like your dad," Ali said, smiling. "Your dad kept talking about you, little man. Did you have a good flight? I am sure you must be tired. Let me help you with the suitcase."

Ali was very handsome, tall, in his early thirties. He had curly black hair and big dark- brown eyes with long lashes. He was a college student, studying political science and working as an English teacher.

"We have to take the bus to get to Ankara. I am sorry to tell you, but it is a long drive. I know you are really tired, but maybe you can take a nap," Ali told us.

Ali sat next to Cyrus, right behind Azeeta and me. I could hear him talking to Cyrus, asking questions, trying to keep him occupied, so he wouldn't get restless. It made me feel really good to know that he cared about us. I felt that even though my brother was physically gone, his spirit was present.

It *was* a long drive from Istanbul to Ankara—about eight hours—so I didn't even notice the shabbiness of Ali's neighborhood or apartment when we arrived. Ali shared the apartment with his girlfriend, Tonia. Two of his male friends, Akbar and Hassan, were also staying there, also waiting to get their visas to go to America.

Ali took our suitcases to one of the bedrooms with a queen-sized bed. "I think the bed is big enough for all three of you," he told me with a friendly smile. "You don't worry about anything, Soodabeh. Just think of me as your brother. We will go to the American embassy tomorrow morning. Don't worry, please. Everything will be okay. I will do anything to help you, I promise. Please feel free to rest a little. I am going to make dinner."

"Oh, my God, thank you Ali for being so wonderful and generous. How can I ever thank you?"

"Well, you can help me to go to America when you get there."

"Absolutely. Just pray I get there, and I promise to help you."

I woke up to the sound of a gentle knock on the bedroom door. I got up and started to get everyone ready and made breakfast for everyone.

We still made it to the embassy before eight. There was a long line of people in front of the building.

"Wow, so busy so early. I hope you don't have to go anywhere, Ali."

"Hey, don't you worry about me at all. I told you, I will do whatever it takes, remember? No worries allowed here," he said, laughing.

It was cold and exhausting, waiting for hours to get inside with two young kids. I was so glad for Ali, who played with Cyrus, running and jumping up and down.

Finally, we got in, and Ali submitted our paperwork to the immigration officer, explaining my situation and the reason we were there.

"Okay, you have an appointment to come back in six weeks," said the officer.

I felt very disappointed to hear that.

"Yes, unfortunately, it takes a long time," Ali said. You are welcome to stay with me as long as you need to. I am not going to be home most of the time, as I work during the day and go to school at night.

To thank Ali, I cooked and cleaned for Tonia and him. Though I saw that work as my rent, he saw it as a gift.

"Thank you, Soodabeh. It was delicious, as usual," he would say. "You are spoiling me. What will I do when you leave?"

Tonia was fluent in two languages, Turkish and Kurdish, and knew a little English. I knew a little of all three, and with the use of an English dictionary, we were able to understand each other most of the time. It was so much fun to have someone to talk to and laugh with, finally.

Tonia was gorgeous, tall, and physically fit. She had long, wavy blond hair, all the way to her mid back, big blue eyes with long lashes, and the most beautiful smile. She was sweet, loving, gentle, and always smiling. She loved to play guitar and sing with a beautiful voice. She would sing and play for me, trying to make me feel comfortable and ease my pain. However, a few days later, Tonia had to move to another city to go back to college. It was so hard for me to imagine staying there without Tonia.

"I am sorry I have to leave. I love you and the kids so much. I know I will miss all of you." She gave me a hug and kissed Cyrus and Azeeta before leaving.

It was really hard for me when Tonia left. Her presence had made me feel safe, and her absence left me lonely and scared. The following week, Akbar got his visa and left Turkey too.

I noticed that the food I had brought with me was almost gone, leaving me to wonder how to feed my children. I had no choice but to call Hameed.

"How much are you eating?" he asked. "It's only you and the kids."

"No, it's not just me. I had to prepare food for Ali, his girlfriend, and his friends."

"Well, I don't know what to tell you. You can't spend any money. You need it for the ticket here."

I knew that I had to spend some of the money I had. Although I couldn't afford to buy meat or fruit, I was able to buy bread, cheese, eggs, and vegetables. I would cook breakfast and lunch only for my children, but I felt obligated to cook dinner for Ali every night, since he was helping me a lot. It was important that I could trust him and feel safe knowing he would be there for me no matter what.

I decided to make food for Cyrus and Azeeta and hide it under our bed so Hassan couldn't see or eat it. It made me feel guilty at first, but it was my only choice. Most of the time, I didn't eat anything.

Ali's apartment was on the fourth floor in a run-down part of the city. It was common for us to lose power or for the water to be turned off for hours at a time. When there was water, it wasn't hot, as there was no water heater. I had to boil water in several pans in order to bathe.

Our bedroom did have a small balcony facing the mountain, a beautiful view that offered my only comfort. Two gray pigeons with colorful wings, like the rainbow, visited every day.

I think these beautiful birds are guardian angels, sent by God. They must be the spirit of my dad and Soson, coming to comfort me, telling me they are here, watching, and protecting me. I would talk to them as if they could understand me. "Please, pray for me so I can get out of here soon," I would say, crying. I was depressed, lonely, and desperately in need of divine intervention.

Six weeks passed by very slowly, each day seeming as long as a year. I prayed every day that I wouldn't get sick, because of the way

I was eating, or not eating. Finally, the day of my appointment came. This time, we didn't have to wait long.

"Did her husband send any documents to us before?" the officer asked Ali.

"I don't know, sir. We don't think so."

"Let me go check to see if there is anything in our file."

He came back after a few minutes, holding a big yellow envelope, and while taking the documents out of it, he looked at Ali and said, "Yes, we have these records. You didn't need an appointment. I wish you would have told us you had a file here. Everything is ready for you, except the medical exam."

Ali looked at me with a beautiful smile, trying to translate what the officer said.

"I understood what he said, Ali. We are going to America. Oh, my God, finally." I was trembling inside with excitement, tears of joy running down my face. I started hugging and kissing Cyrus and Azeeta.

"Ali, you are a wonderful man. I don't know how to thank you, but I know I will pray for you, day and night. God bless you, Ali. You really are an angel. Thank you."

Ali started hugging me, crying. "Soodabeh, I didn't do anything for you. God loves you very much, believe me. I honestly thought you would be here for at least a year. I decided not to tell you, knowing you would freak out."

"I am going to buy chicken and rice to make dinner tonight. We deserve to eat a decent meal," I told Ali.

After a couple of weeks, we went back to the immigration office with the results of our medical exams, our photos, and all the necessary documents. I finally got my visa after fifty days of pain and suffering in Turkey.

"It's my turn to buy dinner tonight, and to show you the city. You will be leaving me soon," Ali said.

I had to call Hameed to tell him the good news.

"I managed to get a loan from Reza. I got the tickets for you. Don't spend any money. I have to pay this loan as soon as possible."

I didn't want to be in Turkey any longer, and I was excited to finally be going to America to join my husband.

The day before our flight to America, I bought chicken to make dinner one last time. I cooked the chicken in the evening right before Ali came home, poured the broth in a large bowl, and put it in a corner on the kitchen floor. It was a very small kitchen with little counter space.

The aroma brought Cyrus and Azeeta into the kitchen.

"I made your favorite," I told Cyrus. "Chicken with rice."

"Oh, I want some! I want some!" he said, jumping up and down with excitement.

Azeeta, reached her hands to me. "Are you hungry, baby? Oh, my love, how about a little piece?"

I gave her a piece of chicken, put her down, and turned away to get some for Cyrus too. Cyrus started arguing with Azeeta for the chicken.

"Give it to me! I want that!" Cyrus yelled at his sister.

Before I had time to say one word or even turn around with Cyrus's piece, I heard Azeeta scream in terror. I turned, thinking I was going to stop a sibling fight, but I saw Azeeta sitting in the bowl of hot chicken broth. Azeeta had lost her balance when Cyrus was trying to grab the food from her.

I grabbed her, stood her up, and started pulling her pants and diaper off, when I noticed that her skin was coming off with the pants from her lower back, her bottom, thighs, and all the way down to her ankles.

"Oh, my God, help! Please, somebody help me! Oh God, oh God!"

"What is going on?" Hassan came running.

"She is burned! I need to take her to the hospital!" I cried hysterically.

"Let's go to the pharmacy across the street. They may know what to do," he said, trying to calm me down.

Hassan held Cyrus's hand and I carried Azeeta on her stomach, trying not to put any pressure on the burned area.

Azeeta continued to scream, making me more nervous and frightened, and I was unable to calm her down. "Please, baby, Mom is here."

"Here," the pharmacist said. "Just give her this suppository. It will reduce the pain until you take her to the hospital."

Hassan and I didn't know where the hospital was, so I had no choice but to wait until Ali came home.

When Ali got home and saw us, he flew into action, grabbing Cyrus and running outside to get us a cab. There were too many patients in the emergency room. Azeeta had calmed down since I had given her the suppository. However, Cyrus was shaking and crying quietly.

"Come on, buddy. She is going to be okay. Don't worry, Cyrus." Ali kept talking to Cyrus, trying to calm him down.

We were still waiting for the doctor when I noticed that Azeeta's eyes were rolling backward, and her tongue was protruding out the left corner of her mouth, and she was drooling. Her breathing was shallow and very slow.

"Oh, my God, please help. She is having a seizure. Please, get the doctor here now!" I yelled, but no one paid any attention. Everyone was busy with other patients.

"What is it, Soodabeh?" asked Ali, running toward me from where he and Cyrus had been sitting.

"She is having a seizure. Oh, my God, she is not breathing! Please, she needs oxygen—she needs a doctor right away!" I was screaming. "Please, at least give her oxygen! My daughter is dying here!"

Cyrus started praying, "Please, God, don't let her die. I will never do that again." I could hear my son praying and begging for her sister's life.

Finally, a nurse ran in with oxygen. I was unable to do anything for my daughter—her little face was covered by the mask and her body was so lifeless—but to pray. However, after a few minutes, I began to see she was breathing normally, and she slowly opened her eyes.

"Oh, my baby. She is getting better. Oh, thank God, she is alive! Cyrus, honey, she is okay. Come here, baby," I reached for Cyrus and kissed him.

I knew that it wasn't just the oxygen that brought her back. I believed with all my heart and soul that it was our prayers, once again, especially Cyrus's.

Azeeta had had an allergic reaction to the suppository. The doctor told me that it was supposed to have been removed from the pharmacies a few months ago. He was surprised we were given that. It was truly a miracle she didn't die, the night before our flight to America.

Azeeta had first- and second- degree burns from her lower back down both of her legs. The doctor cleaned the burned area, wrapped it with white gauze, and secured it with tape.

"Here, take these extra supplies with you, just in case you need them. Make sure to take her to the hospital the minute you arrive there in America," the nurse told us.

We woke up early in the morning after sleeping only a few hours. We were all emotional, still drained from the night before and feeling excited yet nervous about the trip. It would be a long journey, up to thirty hours with several layovers. I was worried whether Azeeta would tolerate the long flight. I wasn't going to tell anyone that she had been burned the night before; I was afraid they might not allow us to leave.

"I am going to miss you very much. Please don't forget me," Ali told us, holding Azeeta in his arms. "Remember it is my dream to go to America." He hugged Cyrus and kissed him good-bye.

"Please write to me," he said, shaking my hands.

"Ali, that is the first thing on my list, I promise you."

CHAPTER 10

I walked down the aisle of the airplane overwhelmed with emotions. This was really it, the end of one part of my life and the beginning of another. Soon enough, I had to think about practical matters, such as concealing Azeeta's condition from the flight attendants. I carefully sat her in the window seat. To my surprise, she sat calmly with an angelic smile, which made me relax a little.

"Are you okay, baby? We are going to see Daddy."

"Mom, Mom," Cyrus tugged on my shirt.

"What is it, honey?"

"We are going to see Dad, Mom?" Oh, I am so happy. I miss him so much."

Azeeta and Cyrus slept most of the time during that first flight. As we touched down for a three-hour layover in Germany, Cyrus started bouncing in his seat.

"Where is Dad, Mom?"

"No, honey, this is Germany, another country. We have to wait here for a while to take another flight to go to America."

"Wow, another one? It's so cool. Right, Mom?"

"Yes, baby, it is. You are such a wonderful son. I love you so much. You have been helping me and your sister a lot. I am very proud of you, Cyrus."

While waiting for our flight, I kept thinking about Soson and my family in Iran. I was on my way to see my husband after three years. My heart was heavy, wishing Soson was there to see it, to share this beautiful moment with me. And, it was time to board again. The next time we landed, I heard the words I'd been dreaming of:

"Welcome to America. May I see your passport?" the immigration officer in the airport asked me with a smile.

I must have looked like I had been dreaming of this moment, because he went on.

"Is it your first time here?"

"Yes, sir. I came to join my husband after three years."

"Where are you headed to?"

"We are going to Portland, Oregon."

"Okay, have a safe trip."

We boarded for a third and final time on this journey. We had one more layover in Seattle, but we didn't have to change planes there. At 3 a.m., we finally arrived in Portland. I allowed myself to think about being reunited with my husband—his touch, the sound of his voice, his warmth beside me every night in bed.

As we rounded the corner to the gate, I saw Hameed, Reza, and Maryam with her husband Shahab. I had been fantasizing about seeing him and had imagined him running to hold me in his arms and kiss me.

Shahab ran with arms wide open, grabbed Azeeta, and put her on his shoulder, jumping up and down with excitement.

"Not so hard with her!" I said, but I couldn't help laughing. Maryam came toward me, her arms open to hug me.

I started crying the minute I saw her.

"That's okay, Soodabeh. You are here. No more tears for you, my dear. We are glad to see you and the kids."

Finally, Hameed came and hugged me quietly.

I filled them in on Azeeta's journey. "We need to take her to the hospital to have her dressing changed by a nurse."

"Okay. Shahab and I will go with you," Hameed said. "Maryam, can you take Cyrus with you?"

When we got to the emergency room, Hameed went to the receptionist and gave them his information. Shahab was happy and excited, talking to me about the trip and asking questions about the incident that brought us to the hospital. After many hours of waiting, they called our name.

"I will translate for you," Shahab told me kindly. "Come on, little girl, it's our turn," Shahab said to Azeeta, holding her in his arms. "Uncle Shahab is here. You are going to get better soon, I promise."

"Thanks. You are as kind and loving as you have always been, Shahab," I said.

The nurse saw no signs of infection and gave us more dressings, and we were cleared to go home.

We finally got there, my new home—our apartment. The sun had not yet risen, so I couldn't see my new city. I was just glad I was with my family.

Hameed parked in the driveway and then gathered up Cyrus. I followed him with Azeeta, up the cemented steps and through the light blue wooden door. Although I was exhausted, I was grateful to finally make it home.

PART 2

MY NEW LIFE IN AMERICA

CHAPTER 11

I woke up early in the morning. Cyrus and Azeeta were still sleeping. I took a shower and made breakfast. There was a square dining table and four golden-brown metal chairs in the kitchen by the window, which offered a beautiful view of large trees.

I dropped into one of the chairs and let my eyes go out of focus as I looked at the green, orange, and yellow leaves shining in the rain. I was hoping for Hameed to come and hold me in his arms, kiss me, and tell me that he loved me very much. I wanted to hear what he used to write in his love letters to me, promising a beautiful future.

But instead, I continued to sit there, alone, staring aimlessly out the window. I was in my new home, a small one-bedroom apartment. I was lonely and frightened with an uncertain future: I was alone with two young children.

I don't have money, I don't have family or friends, I can't speak English, I don't know how to get anywhere. How am I going to survive?

I realized there was only one way. I had to move forward, get my life back together, and succeed. Going back to Iran was completely out of the question. I was determined to create a better life for my family.

No, it can't be. I waited three years to come here and to have a better life. I want to forget all the pain and suffering I have experienced and focus on a wonderful, happy future. I am not going to focus on the fear and worry.

In that moment, I felt the lost warrior in me coming out, lending me a shield, and encouraging me to fight the battle. I was determined with every ounce of my being to fight and to succeed with victory.

I kept praying, *Please, dear God, give me the strength to take care of my family. You are my only hope.* Although I could not see the light at the end of the tunnel, I had faith, and somehow I knew that I would survive.

The sound of Cyrus and Azeeta's laughter brought me back to reality. Finally, I called out, "Come on, guys, breakfast is ready."

"Okay, Mom, we are coming," Cyrus said, laughing.

I got Azeeta up and sat her in a chair.

I heard a footstep followed by a knocking on the door. Shahab brought us a Christmas tree and many colorfully wrapped boxes of ornaments. He stood in the doorway with his hands on his hips, smiling ear to ear, watching the kids jump up and down with excitement.

"Oh, my God, Shahab. Thank you so much. You didn't have to do this. I am so grateful for you and everything you have done for us."

"Well, I thought you have no one to do anything for you. I wanted them to remember their first Christmas here."

"Thank you so much."

"Okay, kids. Where are my hugs and kisses? I've got to go back to work."

Cyrus and Azeeta started decorating the tree with red, blue, gold, and green ornaments and shaking their gifts.

"Do you need help?" I asked.

"No, I know how to do this," Cyrus said. "Azeeta, come here. Can you give one to me?"

I was thrilled to see them so happy and strong.

"Mom, could we just open our presents now?"

"No, people open their presents on Christmas Day."

"But I want to know what there is."

"I know, but we have to wait. Make sure Azeeta doesn't touch them either. After you are done decorating, we will put them on the floor under the tree. Do you remember when we went to the store? There were lots of gift boxes under the tree. We have to do the same thing. This is the tradition."

Although I was unable to imagine a bright, happy, and successful future, I knew the days of staying at home and feeling sorry for myself were over. I had a goal—to make sure I could provide a better life for my family and me. I was looking forward to going to school, learning English, and making friends.

We had arrived in America in November, so Cyrus missed the first quarter of the school year. He was, therefore, more than ready to start first grade shortly after the New Year. I was nervous to take Cyrus to school, not knowing how to communicate with his teacher or other parents. However, I was excited to try, and I was a proud mom, realizing he had grown up so.

Well! Cyrus was very smart, and he made friends and learned English quickly. He looked forward to going to school every day and coming home to teach Azeeta what he had learned there.

By walking Cyrus to school, I met our next door neighbor, Tim, a tall and sturdy African American man, who also walked his two children, Kathy and Dana, to school; they were the same ages as Cyrus and Azeeta.

"Come visit us some evening to meet my wife, please," Tim said as we parted.

Oh, thank God, I thought. *He was so nice, not making fun of me and trying to explain so patiently, making sure I understood what he had said, instead.*

Before I could get to their house to introduce myself to Tim's wife, Linda was knocking on my door that very night. It meant so much that they wanted to get to know me. Soon, Kathy and Dana were coming over after school to play with Cyrus and Azeeta. It was wonderful to see them with friends, and it was the perfect way for them to learn English.

CHAPTER 12

I found a wonderful babysitter, Nickle, a few blocks from the apartment. She and her husband had two school-age children of their own, and Nickle was watching four young children when we met her. Her big blue eyes shone with so much light and joy as we sat at the table overlooking her colorful garden.

"I am worried that Azeeta can't speak English. I am not sure if she could communicate her needs," I said.

"Well, why don't you tell me some words she might use for needing to use the bathroom, being hungry, and thirsty, etcetera?" Nickle asked, pulling out a pen and paper.

It is a miracle, I thought. *I have met wonderful neighbors, great teachers at Cyrus's school, and now the most amazing woman to babysit my child while I go to school. Thank you, God. You have brought so many angels into my life already. I know this is your way of saying you are here to watch over me, isn't it?*

The bus stop for the bus that would take me to school was about two miles from Nickle's house. Feeling butterflies in my stomach for my first day of school, I tried to focus so I wouldn't miss my stop. I recognized the little market on the north corner of the street. I got off and walked another mile.

I sat in the front of the classroom. As the teacher walked in, I noticed her soft black hair and big brown eyes. Melinda was very sweet and thoughtful.

"I am so happy you are here. We need to talk. How about after class?" she said when she heard my story.

Melinda and I talked after the class about my new life in America. She was very intrigued to find out I had been a nurse in Iran. "Soodabeh, this is the perfect place. This college has a great nursing program. Would you like me to take you to talk to one of the advisors?"

"Yes, that's awesome. Thank you, Melinda. You are an angel!"

After we made an appointment in the advising office, I left school in a very good mood. As I cooked dinner, I realized that I had many options. Shahab was right. Separating from Hameed was the best thing for me. If I'd stayed with him, I would have continued to depend on him, and then I would have missed opportunities. I felt as if I had been reborn, and like a baby, I was learning how to talk and walk and make the new decisions I needed to make. Sometimes the progress felt slow, but it always felt good. I could at least see progress, finally.

My good mood continued the next day, at the meeting with the advisor.

"You already have a one-year degree," Linda said. "So you can take the board exam, and if you pass, you will be able to start working as a practical nurse. However, this college has a great nursing program. You can become a registered nurse in two years. The Bridge to Success Program here is designed to help minorities succeed in school. Being a single mom of two children, new to this country, you are eligible for financial aid, work study, and a low-interest loan."

Ten years after I started my schooling to become a registered nurse, I could actually complete my degree?

I remembered what Shahab had told me a few weeks before. *You will survive and succeed if you want to.* He was right. God had better plans for me.

With the help of an English tutor, Steve, who was also from Iran, I passed Melinda's class, and she suggested I skip to the advanced class the following term.

Being able to communicate better in English not only increased my confidence and kept my education on the fast track but also it allowed me to connect with people who knew exactly what I was going through. My classmates were from all over the world, so English was our common language; some had been here a long time, and some were new like me. All were willing to reach out and offer helping hands.

Kim, originally from Korea, became a good friend. She was in her mid-sixties, divorced but with a boyfriend, with adult children and grandchildren.

"I have been here for many years, since I was a teenager," she told me. "I got married, raised my children—all of them successful, married, and with children of their own. I went to school many times to learn to write in English, but I haven't been able to do so. As you see, I can talk and read, but I am unable to write. I wanted to work as a waitress, but I couldn't write down the orders. That's the reason I am taking this class. I will succeed at writing in English this time."

As spring in Portland bloomed, I felt a bit melancholy. March 21st is the Iranian New Year, the most important holiday. Normally, I would be celebrating for two weeks, exchanging gifts, and indulging in elaborate dishes. But this first New Year without Soson and all of my family, I was homesick. I couldn't stop thinking about my niece, nephew, and my sister-in-law, living without Soson. They had no idea I was separated from Hameed. I couldn't tell them what had happened, since they were still mourning the loss of Soson. I preferred they think I was living a happy life with him.

Though I was tormented with grief, going to school kept my mind occupied, gave me purpose each day, and my faith in God and the constant help of my friends helped me to move forward, gradually. As spring drew to a close, I found that I agreed with Cyrus, who said he wasn't looking forward to summer vacation because he would miss school and his friends. I would miss my classes and friends, too!

"They have tutors in the downtown library," Nickle told me when I confessed that I wished school was all year. "It's free. You can take a bus there."

"Oh, thank you, Nickle. You are a life saver."

I met Jeff only two days later. He was in his early twenties, born and raised in Portland. He was tall and handsome, with blond hair, blue eyes, and the most beautiful smile.

"I just graduated college. I majored in English literature and plan to be a teacher in Hong Kong at the end of summer," Jeff explained softly. "Tell me about yourself, please. What is your plan?"

"I am a single mom with two children. I was a nurse in Iran and would love to be able to work here soon. I am planning to start taking college-credit classes in the fall and hope to enroll in the nursing program shortly after."

"Oh, that's wonderful. You'll be very successful. Let's plan to get together three times a week for a few hours in the afternoon. Is this going to work for you?"

"Yes, actually. It's perfect. I can take care of the kids in the morning and take them to the babysitter before I meet you here."

Jeff was an amazing teacher. He pushed me to work hard, yet he was very gentle and patient. "Wow, you are the perfect student, always challenging me to work harder and to be a better teacher. You are quick, smart, and intelligent. You will be very successful. Trust me, you have nothing to worry about. I am very pleased to be working with you."

I was thrilled by his motivating words.

"I am intrigued by your story, Soodabeh," he told me. "You have done a great job writing essays so far. Do you mind going further, writing something about your own life experiences?"

"Yes, I think so."

I believed he was another angel sent by God. *I know it's not just a coincidence to have him as a teacher,* I thought.

CHAPTER 13

Part of the school financial aid I received included work-study. While I was studying the job board, the receptionist pointed out a position for an English tutor. "You should do this," she said.

"I am still trying to learn English. I don't think I can help anyone yet."

"Why not? You speak very well. They are students like you. English is not their native language. Remember when you started? You would be perfect for them, since you have experienced that."

"Are you serious? You really think I can do this?"

"Listen, I don't have time to convince you. Do you want it or not?"

"Yes, I am sorry. I will take it."

I was nervous, but I was also feeling confident in general early in this fall term because I was doing well in my classes. I got an A on my first biology test. Unfortunately, a shot of lack of confidence was walking my way, literally.

I was so grateful and blessed to be able to go back to school and even work there. Being able to communicate with others was liberating for me. I was given the opportunity of a lifetime, being born again, feeling young and vibrant with more energy and stamina.

We moved closer and closer to Christmas and Cyrus's birthday. I was surprised when a gift arrived for all of us.

"Open the door," came a familiar voice from outside one night. "It is Uncle Shahab."

The kids ran to the door, and there was Shahab with a large TV and a VCR.

"Oh, Shahab, you didn't need to do this," I said. "How could I ever thank you?"

"This is nothing. It is time to get rid of that stupid little TV. It irritated me every time I looked at it," he said, laughing. "Now you can watch movies, too."

Life would not always be perfectly smooth, but this was all right, I decided. I invited some of Cyrus's friends for his birthday and made sure he was having a great day. I didn't wanted to miss my son's birthday because it was one week before Christmas. I wanted him to know that his birthday was a special day for us all. Watching my family happy was the best gift for me.

After the holidays, I started taking more challenging classes, such as microbiology and advanced reading and writing. I was completely focused on my studies and determined to succeed, and I was looking forward to starting the nursing program soon. Although it was very hard, by persistence and hard work, I was able to pass that term with great grades. My classmates and teachers were amazed at my progress.

"How do you do that Soodabeh?" one of my classmates, Sam, asked me one day. "How could that even be possible that you not only passed the microbiology, but you got a good grade?"

"I don't know," I said laughing. "I don't have a life, I guess. All I do is read and take care of my children."

That was the truth. I would study past midnight most nights. I had no choices and had no one to rely on. That was the only thing that could help me provide the life I have always dreamed of. I wasn't afraid of working hard. Compared to the life I had in Iran—working long hours and with only two days off per month—this was heaven. Going to school and studying didn't even seem challenging to me.

The next Iranian New Year, I didn't feel the homesickness I had felt the year before; instead I felt the rebirth and renewal the holiday called for. My self-confidence and sense of self-worth had significantly increased. I had fought many battles, one after another, and survived all the challenges.

Because of that, I knew I could address my current concern. My timing was off with school. I'd finish my nursing school prerequisites right after the deadline for applying had passed, meaning I'd have to wait a whole extra year to start nursing school. But I'd been doing very well in my classes; I was a part of the Student Success Program, which supported minorities in nursing, and my accolades were well documented there—and I had many years of experience as a nurse in Iran. I decided to talk to the director of the nursing program.

I thought I would need to make an appointment, so I was surprised when the receptionist told me the director was available to see me right then. Maureen, as she introduced herself, was gorgeous, dressed in a black pantsuit, her brown wavy hair pulled back in a ponytail, and her smile was very friendly.

"I am sorry for the negative things you have experienced so far," she said, after I told her my story, "and I'm proud of you for your accomplishments. To tell you the truth, you are bold, thinking you can enter the program and take other classes in addition to the nursing ones. This is a very intense program, and many students drop out."

"I promise I will make it. I am not afraid of hard work, and I will do whatever it takes."

I wasn't ready to take no for an answer.

Leaning back in her chair, she looked at my transcript and then looked back up at me. "There is a bridge program for licensed practical nurses during the summer. This can prepare you for the second year of nursing school. You could do that."

"Yes, I will do whatever you ask me to."

Her eyes lit up. "I have never met anyone like you, Soodabeh. I am sure you will be very successful. Please let me know if there is anything I can help you with." She stood up to shake my hand and walk me out the door.

I was on top of the world. Even though I was working a lot between classes and taking care of my family, I was happier than I had ever been. I felt like the luckiest woman on earth. I had peace in my life, I had my children, and I was able to go to school. What else did I need?

"Soodabeh, why are you happy all the time? You are single, and all you do is work, go to school, and take care of the kids. How do you do that?" Nickle would ask me, laughing and making fun of me sometimes. "Please, go, have a date, dinner, or something. You are young. Go enjoy your life."

"I am enjoying my life. That's why I am happy and smiling. Trust me, I am never again going to date or be in a relationship."

"Not all men are the same, Soodabeh. I was married before. Look at my husband now. He is the best, gentlest, kindest, most loving and generous man I have ever known. He even adopted my children."

"I know, and I am happy for you. But I have to focus on school right now. I don't have time to get distracted."

"I promise to babysit the kids for free if you go to dinner with a man."

"Oh, Nickle, please, just stop it," I told her before leaving her house. I loved her so much. We had become best friends, and I was very grateful to have her in my life.

Although I wasn't in a good situation financially—with student loans, financial aid, and working part-time at school—I was able to survive. My children were growing up and required more clothes, shoes, and many other things. I decided to start babysitting during the evening, and eventually I was able to make some extra cash to spend on the kids. We would go to secondhand stores to buy shoes and clothes or go to fast food restaurants to eat a meal. I had to take care of my family but also make sure they were enjoying life as well.

Plus, being able to do these things brought me another type of joy. Until then, all my decisions had been made by someone else—not only important life decisions but even little ones, like buying clothes. I had to go with either my mother or my husband, who would make sure I had purchased the right color and style! And I was reminded of another thing.

Living in a materialistic world, we are taught that happiness means having more money, owning a big house, buying new cars, and so on. We forget to appreciate the small blessings in life, like being able to walk, talk, and see—and the love of family and friends. I was well aware of my financial situation, but the love and passion I had for life and my family made me believe I was the most successful woman in the world. I was a magnificent being; I was complete.

As part of my nursing program, I had early morning clinical rotations in the hospital twice a week. It was very hard for me to get there before 6:00 a.m., considering I didn't have a car and had to take two to three buses to get there. However, classmates soon became friends, and they willingly would offer to help.

"Sherry," I said to one, "I don't know what I can do for you. You have been the best friend, picking me up early in the morning and taking me home. You don't even live close to me. How am I going to repay you?"

"Don't worry about it, Soodabeh. We all need help sometimes."

Though I was still learning to read, write, and speak English, I had an advantage in that I'd been a nurse already, so I knew all the medical terminology.

"Wow, Soodabeh, how could you even pronounce these words?" my classmates would ask.

We laughed about which was more difficult: English or Latin. My friends also complimented my work. "You amaze me all the time, Soodabeh. You are so fast, changing the dressings and taking care of your patients with so much confidence."

"You will be the same in ten years," I would respond, laughing. What a strange thing, to be a nurse back in nursing school!

While most people were happy for me and believed I deserved to be there, there were others who acted superior and believed I shouldn't have been allowed to start the program before finishing my prerequisite classes.

The nursing program was very challenging for me. I had difficulty taking the tests and understanding the questions sometimes. It affected me so badly that at one point I thought I would fail the program.

"Soodabeh, I suggest you go see one of the advisors who is trained in techniques to help you succeed," Linda suggested.

I left her office and went straight to talk to one of the college advisors, Natasha. She was sitting, looking down, looking at a book on her lap, and her curly, dark blond hair shielded her face. She stood up when I said hello, her light gray pantsuit smoothing into place, and she offered her hand.

Natasha listened attentively to my concerns, and after I was finished she smiled and said, "I know how to help you. Have you heard anything about guided imagery or visualization techniques?"

"No, I haven't."

"Well, I guess you are going to learn today," she said with a sweet smile.

"Close your eyes and relax, trying to take several deep breaths." Her voice became even more gentle and soothing. "Now, imagine you are in the most beautiful place, surrounded by many exquisite, colorful flowers, just like a paradise. Smell the salty air. You can see the sun shining and hear the birds singing as you walk down a small path toward a white building with glass windows. Standing there, you see a white paper, with names and grades written in black ink, taped on one of the windows. There it is. You can see your grades posted on the white paper. 'Yes!' you say, feeling excited, knowing that you passed. You did it, you succeeded, and you are on your way to go celebrate."

Though I felt very calm and relaxed, I wasn't sure how it would help me pass the actual test.

"We need to have a few more sessions. Would you like to make another appointment?"

I was glad I did, despite my doubts. I noticed that the more I practiced the exercises with Natasha, the more relaxed I felt. I was able to focus better, and gradually my fears vanished and my grades improved. Visualization surprised me with its effectiveness.

Although my test scores improved, and I proved my abilities to the director of the nursing program and my advisors by passing my tests, I was terrified to hear some of the other students had quit the program.

I am not going to fail. This is my life and dream. I have two children to support. I am not going to give up or quit, I kept thinking.

I was able to finish the term gracefully. I had learned to be strong, believe in myself, and not to ever consider quitting or giving up on my dreams. The challenges I faced made me stronger every day.

CHAPTER 14

Summer arrived, greeting us with beauty and fun. Although it was more difficult to complete the condensed summer term—which was six weeks instead of twelve—I was happy to be able to spend some time with my family. We didn't have money to travel, but we were satisfied to spend time playing in the park, going on the water slide, and swimming.

Cyrus was always inquisitive and exceptionally smart. He loved books; once I saw him attempting to read even my textbooks.

"What are you doing, Cyrus?" I asked, watching him sit at the dining table, my book open in front of him, a pen in his hand and a notebook beside him.

"I am reading, Mom."

"You are reading my book?"

"Yes, Mom. You know I can read, right?" he responded, laughing. I loved the sound of his laughter and the way his little black eyes would disappear in a squint.

"I know you can read, baby. But do you understand?" He reminded me of when I was young, the same age as him, and reading my father's books.

"Of course. We learn this at school. It's science. I am learning about the virus."

"Really? Do you like science?"

"I love science. I am going to take this drawing I made of a virus to show my teacher and friends when we go back to school."

"Are you going to be a doctor?"

"I think so. I want to be a brain surgeon."

"Wow, you are very ambitious! I am very proud of you, Cyrus. You are the best son," I told him while holding him in my arms and kissing his face.

I couldn't believe it. My son had grown up so fast, trying to read and learn my books.

Cyrus was also very supportive and protective of Azeeta. It would irritate her, sometimes, though.

"You are not the boss of me, Cyrus," she would object with a frown, her little hands on her hips.

They would argue and fight like other kids, making me angry. When I raised my voice trying to discipline them, both of them would get mad at me.

"I have to make you guys stop, or I am going to go crazy. If you love each other so much, then stop fighting."

I was human, imperfect with emotions, and exhausted, facing the challenge of going to school, working part-time, staying up at nights to study, and taking care of the children. Sometimes I wished I had someone to help me take care of my kids, so I could study in peace and quiet. I didn't have time to rest or relax, as I was constantly doing something. I would cry sometimes, feeling suffocated in a small room with no air to breathe. I wanted to run away, far, far, from the reality, the challenges I had to endure, but there was no way out. My children were my inspiration and had taught me so much over the years, yet I wished there was a manual to teach us how to be good parents!

Summer was over soon, and I couldn't believe I was about to start the second year of the nursing program.

"This year is very difficult and challenging. You need to work harder and study more," our advisors and instructors would constantly remind us. "It's in your best interest to have study groups, discuss the subjects, and learn together. This helped many students in the past."

I had made many wonderful friends, but Marsha, only a few years younger than me, a nurse in her home country of the Philippines and also a single mother of a three-year-old son, Mathew, was my best friend. She had moved to America a few years before to join her family and was living with them. She was exceptionally kind, loving, and very generous—always willing and eager to offer a helping hand.

"Soodabeh, do you want to join my study group?" she asked one day.

"No, I don't learn that way. I have to read the book at my own pace."

"Okay, no problem. I will go to the study group and you and I can talk about it later.

That way you'll have time to read, and I get more practice with the information."

"You are a genius! Why don't you bring Mathew to play with Cyrus and Azeeta while you go to the study group? I can make food and we can eat when you come back." Being social with each other was not unusual. Marsha had a car and often took us places we had never seen before.

"Yes, sounds great," Marsha said.

"You are the sister I never had," I told her, knowing she was another angel sent by God.

Marsha was very strong and a hard worker. She worked as a nursing assistant at a local children's center at night, taking care of very sick and physically challenged kids. After her shift, she would go home, prepare food for her son, and then go to college after dropping her son off at school.

"Marsha," I asked her one day, "how do you do this? How do you survive working like this, and without adequate sleep?"

"I don't know. I take naps whenever I can." That was true; even while I prepared meals we shared, she would take a nap on the sofa.

One day she asked me, "Soodabeh, can you babysit Mathew? I will pay you."

"Yes, that is a great idea. I need money, and you need a babysitter. Good deal!"

Time went by quickly, and the fall term ended. Marsha and I both passed and looked forward to celebrating the Christmas holidays. She invited the kids and me to join her family for Christmas Day. Though Shahab continued to visit us, I had no contact with Maryam or Hameed. Christmas with Marsha was the first and the best Christmas I had had, and I felt grateful to finally be able to celebrate peacefully.

The next—and the last—two terms were the hardest. I would stay up late at night, trying to keep up with all of my classes.

"Mom, what are you doing?" Cyrus would ask on his way to the bathroom.

"I have to study, honey. I have a test tomorrow."

"But, Mom, it's past midnight."

"I know, honey. You don't worry about me. Please, just go back to sleep."

Cyrus was concerned about me, which I felt bad about, but I also hoped some good would come of him witnessing my hard work and dedication.

Between attending school, working part-time, and taking care of our children, neither Marsha nor I had time for a social life. However, the hard work paid off, and we both passed all of our classes.

"This is it!" Marsha cried enthusiastically. "We get to go pick up our caps and gowns, Soodabeh!"

Two single mothers, and now registered nurses!

Being proud of my accomplishments, I was thrilled to be able to work as a nurse in America. *Thank you, God, for your unconditional love and support. I am truly blessed*, I kept thinking. I was a smart, intelligent, and strong woman. I had achieved my goal and dream of being a registered nurse. And the best part was that I had succeeded without Hameed!

"Sharon and some others and I are going to rent a limousine to go downtown and celebrate after the graduation ceremony," Marsha continued. "My dad can watch the kids until we get home. Do you want to go with us?"

"Yes, I would love to. Oh, Marsha, I am so glad I have you guys in my life," I said, reaching to give her a hug.

Feeling excited and happy to finish school and be surrounded by friends at the graduation ceremony, I did wish my father and brother were alive to witness my success. *I hope you two are proud of me. I know you can see me from up there. I have felt both of you so many times and know you have watched over me, bringing all these wonderful people into my life.* My eyes filled with tears, but this time they were tears of joy and not of sadness or despair.

With my heart beating fast and my legs shaking, I climbed the few steps up the stage to receive my diploma. "This is for all of you— Mom, Dad, Soson, Cyrus, and Azeeta. I am grateful to finally, after experiencing four horrific years, be here. I love you all," I whispered, trying so hard not to shed a tear.

After we all received our diplomas, the dean stepped to the microphone and shouted,

"Congratulations, nursing class of 1994!"

We threw our caps up into the air.

CHAPTER 15

After a few months of searching and failing to find employment as a nurse during the day shift, I took a job as a medical assistant in a doctor's office. My pay was half what I could have made as a registered nurse, but I was happy. I could still support my family, and it would be a great reference for a nursing job. Plus, I was grateful to be working and not going to school anymore.

Within a few weeks, I was able to find another part-time job, and soon I had saved some money to buy a car. In one day, I got my driver's license and a car, with the help of the husband of one of my friends, who owned a used car dealership. I asked Sharon to ask Mike to keep an eye out for a great deal, and she called me back only a few minutes after we had hung up.

"He says to go to the dealership right away," Sharon said.

Thank God for Nickle. I dropped the kids off and rushed to the dealership.

There it was, my first car—a dark red, four-door Pontiac GM.

"What do you think?" Mike said. "It's not a brand new car, but it is very affordable."

"As long as it's safe and drivable, I will sign the papers."

If I hadn't fallen in love with my car on the drive home, I would have after taking one look at my children when they saw it. They jumped up and down with excitement.

"Mom, could we please go for a ride?"

"Sure, let's go!" I tried to hide that I was afraid of driving with the kids in the car.

"Go faster, Mom!"

"You guys need to calm down, please. I just got the car and want to be safe."

Although I could see the disappointment in their eyes, I knew we were all happy not to take a bus ever again. I would take them for a ride in the neighborhood every day after work, and soon I was able to drive without any fears.

My Christmas present to myself in early December was finding full-time employment, a day shift in another nursing home. The kids had other ideas.

"Could we buy lots of toys, Mom?" Cyrus asked with excitement.

I liked the idea. "Yes, of course. We can buy clothes, shoes, toys, and even our own Christmas tree."

"A big tree?"

"Will you be able to carry it?"

"Yes, I can, Mom. I am strong. See these muscles?" He flexed his biceps.

The next step was to move.

"You need to get out of that creepy neighborhood," my friend said. "We are not going to come to visit you until you move closer to us."

I knew they were right. My children had seen drug activities and had once been threatened by a man with a gun.

That day, as usual, I had told them to play right by the apartment. "I need to be able to see you guys."

"But, Mom. It's not fun to stay right here," they both protested.

"Listen, guys. It's not that I don't trust you. There are some crazy people out there, and I am afraid you might get hurt."

"No, Mom. Everybody is nice here. You don't have to worry about us."

I knew I was right, but they didn't believe me until a few weeks later.

"What is going on? You need to calm down. I don't know what you are saying."

Cyrus finally gasped, "There was a man with a big gun. He told us to stop playing there, or he would shoot us."

They had learned their lesson, and so had I—so I was ready for my friend Susan's phone call when it came.

"There is a two-bedroom apartment available in our complex. I have already told my manager about you, and she agreed to rent it to you. Do you want it?" Susan told me.

"Yes, I am ready."

"Okay, then. I can help you pack."

Cyrus and Azeeta were sad to leave their neighborhood friends of five years, yet happy to live in a bigger apartment and have their own bedrooms.

Moving to a new place was very exciting for all of us. Having money to afford new furniture and decorations was refreshing.

"Mom, I love my bed. It's so nice to sleep on a bed, finally," Cyrus said. I hated that my babies had been sleeping on the floor or the sofa in the living room, but that was the past. We had a glorious present.

It felt so good to simply be able to provide for my family. My friends started pushing me to go on a date.

"It's about time you started taking care of yourself. You are done with your school and have a great career, and your kids are growing up," they would say. Maybe they were right.

But I would always find something wrong with the prospects and never liked any of them.

"I don't feel any chemistry," I protested. "I am very happy with my life and not ready for a relationship. I need to focus on myself, trying to find out who I really am." I'd spent so many years in survival mode that I knew it was important for me to just quietly observe my life. Who was I when I wasn't fighting for my spouse's love, providing constant care for young children, and struggling to put food on the table? I no longer had a spouse—or even a manipulative ex—my children were old enough that they preferred to spend time alone or with their friends, and my job was good and secure.

I noticed I enjoyed watching spiritual TV programs. I wanted to learn more about life, the reason for my existence, and the purpose behind all we experience in life. I had so much, but I wasn't happy. There was an emptiness inside, and I was unable to comprehend the reason for it.

I want to know the truth, the reason I am here. What is my life's purpose? What am I going to do for the rest of my life, now that my children are older and don't need me?

I was aware of my intuitive abilities. I had vivid foretelling dreams. I would think of someone one moment, and that person would call me the next—but I didn't know how to utilize this gift to improve my life. For example, I didn't know why I had had the vision when my brother died. I was curious to know. *There must have been a reason to experience that vision, even though I don't understand it.*

"The mind is a powerful tool. You can change your life by focusing on your thoughts," one television program host said, announcing a new book, called *Creative Visualization*, by Shakti Gawain.

Oh, my God. This is what Natasha taught me when I had issues passing the tests a few years ago. I remembered suddenly and was intrigued to learn more about the concept.

"You can create the life you want," the host continued.

I don't want to know the future. I have no control over what I see. I am not ready to deal with another devastating vision, I told myself. But I was just as thirsty and eager to acquire more knowledge about the subject as I was scared, so I decided to buy the book. There was a force within me, guiding me to discover the unknown.

As I continued to ask questions and read more books, practice visualization techniques and meditations, I realized my heightened sensitivity and awareness. I had more vivid dreams; they were more like premonitions. My father, brother, or another deceased family member would reveal important and relevant information about my life, clearly speaking of what I was planning to do, encouraging me to move forward with the appropriate actions. The dreams were clear. I didn't even have to interpret the dreams; I was sure of their exact meaning.

Oh, my God. Is this even possible? I felt confused and scared to get messages in my dreams.

I remembered two of my cousins in Iran were able to communicate with their deceased father through automatic writing. They would hold pens and paper ready, and after they had prayed, their hands would start writing and producing a message, usually a question.

"I don't want to be a part of this, guys," I would tell them, terrified of what they were doing. My mom and aunt encouraged them, missing their loved ones, but I didn't like it at all. "How do you know it's your dad?"

"It is not us writing, for sure. We have no power, as if an unknown force is moving our hands," they would respond gently, trying to reassure me.

They were right, as I could see the handwriting looked different. It was not even close to their own, and sometimes it was very hard to read what they had written.

"I am sorry, but I don't want to play with ghosts or dead people," was always my response, even though I desperately wanted to communicate with my father.

But, this is not the automatic writing, I thought. *I see them in my dreams and know they are talking to me.* It was easier for me to accept them this way. Gradually, I started having visions during the day.

I would be driving or washing the dishes, and all of a sudden I would see a picture in my mind, like I was watching a movie.

I panicked one day when I saw the vision of a police car right in front of my apartment. *Oh, not again. Is this a premonition warning me of danger? Is it about my children? Oh, God, please, kill me now, but keep my kids safe.*

Unfortunately, the vision appeared daily for a while. One early foggy morning, I was driving to work when a cop pulled me over, not far from the apartment.

"Do you know why I stopped you?" the police officer said.

"No, sir, I don't. I was driving the speed limit."

"Your high beams blinded me."

"I am sorry, sir. But it's difficult to see the road."

"That's why you should drive slower, and not the speed limit. I am not going to give you a ticket this time," he said, looking at my nursing badge. "I guess you need to go to work and save lives, right?" he continued, smiling.

"Yes, sir. Thank you." I shook as I continued on to work. *Oh dear God, that must have been it.*

My dreams and visions grew stronger and more powerful. I told no one, unsure what family and friends would think of me.

I started having visions of a new home, a bigger place, one less like an apartment and more like a house. *But how could it even be possible? I am not making enough money to be able to afford a house.*

Thinking about buying my own house was intriguing, making me work more and save more. But I was working in a nursing home and didn't get paid as much as I would working in a hospital.

I miss working in the hospital. Maybe I should start looking for a job there. Maybe I can work on call and on the weekends there. I am sure they need more nurses.

Shortly after I applied, I received the perfect job. I worked Monday through Friday for the day shift in the nursing home and the night shift every other weekend in the hospital. I knew I could count on my friend Susan to take care of the kids when I was working the night shift, since it was only four nights per month.

Although it was very hard having only a few days off every month, thinking of owning my own house motivated me to continue working that way for two years, and I finally bought my first house.

Cyrus and Azeeta were extremely upset and angry for moving again, away from their friends.

"Mom, why are you doing this to us? We don't need a new house. We want to be here and with our friends. We don't want to move again," they protested every day.

"You are growing up, and each of you need your own bedroom. You are not babies any longer, and we all need our own privacy. I know you don't understand it now, but believe me—you will be happier there."

Busy with the new house and shopping for new furniture, I was determined I had found the happiness I had been seeking. However, after a few months I started feeling the dark cloud of loneliness once again. I had no idea what was wrong with me anymore.

"I have accomplished so much and have everything I ever wanted. Why do I still feel so empty? What can I do to feel joy and happiness within my heart? I don't understand what could be missing," I would say to my friends.

"Maybe you can go out dancing with us. You should start socializing with healthy young people. You have been working in a nursing home taking care of sick elderlies, and you're wondering why you are dead inside?" they teased.

"I know. Maybe you guys are right."

I had loved dancing when I was younger. My aunt had taught me to dance when I was only five years old. Although clubs were not part of our culture, we were allowed to dance and have fun at home with the family. Dancing was a part of me, the way I used to express myself. It was very natural and normal for me, thinking everyone was able to move with the music and dance. I used to entertain my children by dancing for them when they were younger.

"Mom, you are funny," they would tell me, laughing loudly, but they also grew to love music.

I was very shy at first, feeling intimidated by so many strangers at the club.

"Go ask that guy to dance," Jackie told me.

"I love to dance, but I am not used to dancing with strange men. I am more comfortable in a group with you guys."

"Yes, we know. But you are here in America, and you need to learn to dance with men, my dear."

"Maybe you need to have a drink and relax first, Soodabeh."

"No, I don't like the taste of alcohol."

"That's okay, you'll get used to it," they said, laughing.

I eased into enjoying going out, and soon I was looking forward to every weekend. And then, after a few months, I met Jason.

I was sitting and watching others dance when he came over.

"Would you like to dance?" Jason asked, looking at me with his beautiful piercing blue eyes.

"Yes, I would love to."

"Wow, you are a great dancer."

"Oh, thanks. I have been dancing since I was a little girl."

"It shows. What is your name?"

"Soodabeh."

He struggled to repeat it.

"It's Iranian. I'm from Iran."

"How long have you been here in America? How come I haven't seen you here before?"

"I have been living here for seven years, but just recently moved to this side of town."

I liked dancing with Jason and looking right into his blue eyes, since he was about my height. Putting my hands on his shoulders, I felt his bulging biceps. He was handsome, polite, and charming. He treated my friends with respect and socialized with them as well.

"What are you drinking?"

"Virgin piña colada."

"No alcohol?"

"No, I don't like the taste of it."

"I used to drink when I would go out. But many years ago, I just decided not to drink anymore," Jason said, before ordering another piña colada for me and iced tea for himself.

It was easy and effortless getting to know Jason. He handed me his business card and said, "I had a great time dancing and talking to you tonight. I hope I hear from you, Soodabeh."

Although I knew I was attracted to him, I felt intimidated about calling him. I had never called a man before. But Jackie encouraged me.

"You don't have to worry about this. Just take the step to call him. He was a gentleman to give you his number. I really think you should, Soodabeh."

I was extremely nervous to call Jason. I kept staring at his business card every day but didn't have the courage to call him.

After a few days, I finally decided to take the first step. I took a deep breath and dialed his number.

"Hi, Soodabeh. How are you? I thought you would never call me," Jason said softly.

"I wasn't sure how to take the first step, I guess. I am from a different culture and still trying to learn how things are done here," I told him.

We laughed together.

CHAPTER 16

Getting to know Jason and his wonderful qualities made me feel like the luckiest woman on earth. We shared many interests, such as being spiritual, believing in God and higher powers, loving dancing, and enjoying working out. We were one soul in two bodies. His great sense of humor was refreshing, and his kindness and generosity made me feel at ease and comfortable around him.

"Where have you been all my life? You are such an amazing woman and bring the best out of me," Jason told me one day.

"Really? I feel the same, Jason."

He kept talking, calling me gorgeous, hot, sexy. I had never heard those words.

"Do you really think I am beautiful?" I kept asking him. "No one has ever told me this before. I am just wondering if you are telling me the truth."

"I am really surprised, Soodabeh. I don't know why you are asking me this, but believe me, I am not lying to you at all."

Jason had twice before been a husband and had two children. I could see the hurt in his eyes, talking about his son.

"He comes to visit me every other weekend, but I want to see him every day, and it's very hard for me to tolerate."

"Please, if you think there is any chance of you guys getting back together, let me know, before it's too late," I asked Jason.

"No. We are waiting for the paperwork. Otherwise, I consider myself divorced," Jason responded. "But don't worry, I want to take it very slow. I have been married twice and divorced twice. Just remember, I want to be with you and get to know you."

Jason and I started talking about God and the angels. It was easy for me to discuss what I believed with Jason.

"I had a vision of me being dead, lying in a coffin with a smile on my face," I told him one day.

"Knock it off! I don't want to hear that," Jason responded, terrified to hear me talking about death.

"But I am not scared. I feel like I am ready any time God wants to take my life. I am worried about Cyrus and Azeeta, but I am not scared of dying." I was really sincere about what I told Jason. I never felt scared seeing that vision, knowing it wasn't a warning about me dying soon. But when it was time to die, I would look happy and content, knowing I would be going home peacefully.

The wonderful feelings started to fade after a few months, however. Although we were still together, dancing and having fun, I noticed that the excitement of a new relationship had disappeared. It was terrifying for me to have disagreements sometimes, making me want to run away. I felt we were drifting apart.

I started reading books to try to understand the reason I was feeling vulnerable. I began to enjoy my space and solitude. Discovering ways to deal with my low self-esteem and insecurities calmed me. A few weeks later, I started having a vision of a car crashing into the right side of mine.

Then as I was getting ready to go to work one day, Azeeta started begging me to stay home. "Please Mom, don't go to work. I had a dream you had a car accident."

I held her in my arms and said, "Honey, I promise to be really careful when I am driving. Nothing is going to happen to me. When I get to work, I will call you and let you know I got there safe." I kissed her and left shortly after she calmed down. Nothing happened that day, and Azeeta forgot all about it. I was terrified to have the vision knowing that Azeeta had had a similar dream, but I decided not to think about it.

I had almost forgotten about the vision myself, when, a few weeks later, with Azeeta sitting in the passenger sit, I got in a car accident.

As I approached an intersection, I noticed the car facing mine had its signal on, waiting to turn left.

I stopped completely. I waited for the other car to turn, but she didn't move at all. *What is she waiting for?* I felt something inside me was telling me to be cautious. I didn't know the warning I felt wasn't about the car in front of me but about the one approaching from my right.

Though the car waiting to turn left saw the silver van coming, I did not. I eased forward, and the next sound I remember was Azeeta screaming.

As I turned to my right to look at her, I heard the loud noise of something crashing into the right side of my car.

I grabbed for Azeeta and cried, "Honey, are you okay? Please, baby, are you hurt?"

She wouldn't stop screaming. People came running toward my car and helped us out through my door. Everyone was worried because the way the car was damaged, we could have been seriously injured, especially Azeeta.

I was searching her body to see if there was anything broken or bleeding, but I only saw minor scratches form the seatbelt, which may have happened when I had pulled her close to me. "Oh, my God. You are okay, baby," I said. I shook as I held her close to me again, trying to comfort us both.

I kept looking at my car and the shattered glass. My beautiful new car. I had bought a brand new Honda Civic about nine months before. I was so proud to be able to afford the car, but now it was gone. I kept wondering why I hadn't seen the van coming down the street. *Maybe some combination of the color of the van and the sun shining in my eyes*, I thought.

The paramedic came soon, and after checking Azeeta and finding her fine, they asked about me. With the shock of the accident and being concerned for Azeeta's safety, I had forgotten to think about my body.

"My neck. It's hurting so bad, and I can't move it," I said.

"Okay. Don't move, please. We have to take you to the nearest emergency room. Do you have any family members to call?"

"Yes. I just called my friend, and he is on his way."

Jason took Azeeta to my friend's home and then met me at the hospital. He arrived soon after I'd been checked out.

"Are you okay?" Jason asked me gently.

"My neck hurts, but I should be able to go home tonight."

"I thought you guys were severely injured when I saw the car. It is a miracle you both survived, but I think your car was totaled."

"I can't believe it. Right before the van hit me, I felt as if we were placed in a bubble. I don't know how to explain what I saw, but I am sure it was divine intervention that protected us from harm. That's the reason we survived."

It took us a long time to get over the accident. I had physical therapy for several months before finally feeling better. Azeeta cried every time I was about to leave the house.

"Mom, please don't leave me. What if you have another accident?"

"I promise you, honey, I will be very careful. I will call you the minute I get to work, okay?"

Jason and I were closer for a short time after the accident. The thought of losing me made him appreciate me more. But it didn't last that long.

"I have good and bad news," Jason told me. I was nervous and didn't know what to say. "I got a promotion. It pays much more than what I am making now. But it is on the east coast. I have to leave soon."

I had no idea what to think, but part of me believed it was good for both of us. Our relationship had come to an end. We had no choice but to accept the fact. I loved Jason. In a lot of ways, he was a wonderful person with a great heart. But, I knew that a long–distance relationship would not work for either one of us.

"I love you, Jason. I want to be with you. But I don't think we can continue. I have a home, a great job, and my children. This is a new relationship for both of us, and we don't know what will happen in the future." I cried.

"I know you do. I hope you know I love you, too."

I started reading lots of books and articles about relationships to learn how to deal with my issues. Although our relationship had come to an end, I wanted to be able to become free from the past and able to move forward. I knew I wasn't ready for any relationship yet.

I was looking for someone to make me feel complete and whole again. I was sick and tired of being unhappy, trying to prove I was a wonderful human being and worthy of being loved. I knew I had to change and learn to love and accept myself. I learned that in order to have a great relationship, I needed to feel loved with who I was. I needed to feel complete on my own, rather than expecting someone else to complete me. I tried to understand the process, but it was difficult for me to feel serenity and inner peace.

My heart was filled with sadness, and I was overwhelmed with excruciating pain, feeling exhausted and hopeless. I became suicidal. I was sick and tired of feeling empty, and nothing was going to fill the void inside.

But the minute I thought about my children, I stopped plotting my death. *I can't leave my children behind, miserable for the rest of their lives,* I realized. I made an appointment to see my primary doctor.

I couldn't stop crying when I saw her, telling her about my depression and suicidal thoughts. "Do you have a plan, Soodabeh?" she asked me.

"I did, but I am not going to do it," I told her.

"May be we should send you to the hospital. I don't feel comfortable sending you home, knowing you already have a plan to kill yourself, Soodabeh."

"But I am not going to do it, I promise. That's why I came here to see you, asking you for help."

"Do you promise not to do anything to harm yourself? I really don't think it's safe for you to go home."

"Yes. I promise, because I love my children and don't want them to suffer."

115

"I am going to prescribe an antidepressant and give you a referral for you to start counseling. Will you do that?"

"Yes, I will do anything to help myself feel better," I said. I promised to make an appointment to go see a counselor the next day.

Taking an antidepressant and going to counseling made me feel better, and at least I stopped thinking about suicide. I started going back to work and pretended I was doing fine. But deep inside I was trying to look for the answer, the reason I had lost control of my life.

I only knew Jason for a year. Why did I fall apart when our very short relationship ended? I wondered.

Although in many ways I did connect this situation with my marriage and divorce, I didn't fully understand I was dealing with those past traumas.

As I continued with the counseling sessions, I realized Jason wasn't the only reason I was angry or depressed.

"I believe you are dealing with the past," said my counselor. "You need to remember no one can make you happy or sad. You are in control of your emotions. You need to take time to grieve the loss of your father, your brother, the tortures you experienced when you were young, and many other issues from the past. Once you are healthy, you will attract the right people into your life."

I knew she was right. I hadn't even had time to grieve for my brother's death or to deal with my divorce. I had tried to ignore that issue by focusing on school and raising my children. I had endured so much pain and trauma but didn't have time or the skills to cope with them appropriately. Finally, my spirit said the toxic relationship was it. I was at the point where I needed to either stop and process my past or die.

I knew I had to focus on myself to get better and healthier.

CHAPTER 17

Determined to achieve a better state of mind and to live serenely and peacefully, I decided to focus on learning from the spiritual masters. I had faith in God to guide me in my journey to find enlightenment. I had been praying to find a great earthly teacher who could work with me and answer my questions.

One day, when I was watching TV, I saw an interview with Doreen Virtue, the author of *Angel Therapy*. She was explaining how to connect with angels and how to hear or see them.

"We have many angels with us all the time. The best way to get to know them is to simply ask them to reveal their names to you. It may be easy for some people, but for others, it may take more practice. Don't be discouraged. They are here to help and guide us," she said.

Feeling very excited, I closed my eyes. *Please, God, help me to see or hear my angels*, I kept praying. But after trying for a few hours of not seeing or hearing anything, I felt disappointed to have failed miserably.

Another day I had a vision of myself dressed in a suit and working in an office. *What is this? I am a nurse and have to wear scrubs to work every day.* The vision continued to pop up in my mind, until I saw a letter in the mail from a pharmaceutical company looking for health care professionals to work for them. *Oh, my God, could that be the reason for what I have been seeing?* I thought, right before picking up the phone and calling the number.

"We are a network marketing company, selling natural and herbal products to prevent disease," said the guy on the phone. "Would you be interested in meeting with me?"

"Yes, I am very interested," I answered. After so many years taking care of patients, especially those going through open-heart surgery, I was eager to learn more about preventative measures and products.

"We encourage our representative to use the products and learn about what they are offering to their clients," Mark explained at our meeting. "You need to invest in the company first by purchasing some products for personal use and to use to promote or distribute. As you sell more products or recruit more people, you'll earn more money."

Although I was surprised to realize I had to spend money to start working with them— having no idea what network marketing was about—I decided to charge my credit card and sign up as a director, anyway. I was fascinated by the products as I started using them myself.

My friends strongly discouraged me, wanting me to stop wasting my time and money, but I never listened. I was constantly talking to people, everybody I knew, encouraging them regarding the benefits of the products, but no one was interested. I was stuck with lots of products in my home but no customers to buy them.

I am not going to give up that easy. I trusted my intuition when I signed up with the company, I thought. I was determined to do anything to succeed. I was very involved, attending all the meetings, wearing suits, as I had seen in my vision, and even going to the international conferences.

I was focused on being a successful businesswoman, making money, and owning my own business. *I know there was a reason for those visions. I have faith and believe I will succeed. I will never give up on this endeavor,* I thought. Despite not making any money with the company, I continued to spend more money and to buy more and more products.

The other sales reps and I used to get together once a week for dinner before the meeting. It was so much fun to be able to sit down and talk to people who shared the same interest. We all loved the products, sharing testimonials about what we had experienced and what we would like to achieve in life. We became very close, like a family, not only discussing the products, but sharing our life stories, thoughts, dreams, and goals.

One of the members of our group was a brilliant man named Bryan. He was a martial arts master and had many degrees in philosophy and psychology, yet was very humble and down to earth. Bryan loved to teach, talking about everything and anything, and made it easy for all of us to feel comfortable sharing our thoughts with him. He became our mentor and counselor, to the point where we started staying in the restaurant after dinner and missing the meetings to ask Bryan for advice.

"Are you guys coming? We are late, waiting for you to start," Mark would say, demanding that we go upstairs to attend the meeting.

"Yes, we are right behind you, Mark," Bryan would tell him, but we never followed him.

"Mark will be really mad at us for missing several meetings," one of us said.

"Don't worry. There are so many people there. He won't notice us not being there," another said, laughing.

One night, we asked Bryan to share something about himself. He was very humble and didn't like to talk about what he had done. He always tried to focus on others, making sure everyone had a good time.

"Well, I have a wonderful girlfriend, Rebeca, and she is a psychic. She communicates with the angels and those who have passed away into the spirit world. She is really amazing at what she does," Bryan told us.

I was so intrigued and excited to hear that. I wanted so much to tell him about my visions right there, but I didn't have the courage to share that with everyone.

"I would love to meet and talk to her someday."

She is going to the Christmas party with me. Are you going?"

"Yes. That's great. I am looking forward to meet her, then."

Although I was eager to talk to Rebeca about what she did, I was nervous once we met at the party. There were so many people, and the mood was too light. We all had so much fun, indulging in the great food and talking casually. However, driving home, I felt disappointed. *I wish I had had the courage to really talk to Rebeca before I left.*

I didn't feel courageous enough to do so for a few months longer. It was March, and my birthday was coming. I had always hated my birthday. *What is the point of getting older if you are not enjoying life or being happy?* But this year, the depression moved me to ask Bryan for Rebeca's number.

He gave me Rebeca's phone number and said, "She'll love to hear from you."

Now I felt I couldn't back out. Bryan knew I had Rebeca's number, and maybe he'd tell her too. So I forced myself to call. Rebeca immediately made me feel safe.

"Would you like to go to lunch and hang out?" she asked.

"Yes, I would love to."

I was not sure how to share my thoughts or feelings with her, but the minute I saw her, I felt serene, and my anxiety vanished, completely. It seemed as if we had been friends for a long time.

"Tell me about yourself, Soodabeh."

I told her about my brother and the visions I had had, my divorce, and the struggles I had experienced. "I want to find some peace and comfort moving on with my life," I explained.

Rebeca listened attentively, and said, "Would you like to check out the bookstore next door? They could help you to learn more about God, angels, and the spirit world."

"I have been praying to have a teacher for a long time, Rebeca."

"Oh, you are very sweet. I am looking forward to working with you, Soodabeh."

Only months before, I had no idea that my life could change so completely, as it was about to. The visions had guided me to the network marketing company, which had led me to Bryan and Rebeca. This would turn out to be a divine intervention and the answer to my prayers.

CHAPTER 18

Rebeca and I met once a week at her office. I trusted that I could tell her everything, without feeling ashamed or guilty. I had worked with a psychologist the year before and didn't want to share anything with her.

"How do you make it so easy and effortless?" I asked Rebeca.

"You are feeling the presence of the angels here. They don't judge. They surround us with unconditional love, guide us to take steps toward our goals and dreams, to improve, and to live a happy life," Rebeca answered.

I had goose bumps, feeling the truth of that statement. It felt very natural, soothing, and safe to work with Rebeca. I never doubted her ability or intentions, knowing my dream of having a wonderful teacher had finally come true.

"In order to connect with angels and the spirit world, you need to meditate. This is the most important part of the journey, and yet it's difficult sometimes," Rebeca explained.

Not thinking about everything going on in my life was not an easy task. In fact, the only time I was able to focus and meditate was when I was with Rebeca.

"I am feeling frustrated not being able to meditate by myself," I told her.

"Everyone has this issue. We are human, after all, and our minds get in the way sometimes. As you practice, you'll see it will get easier. I'm leading a workshop on it in a few weeks. Would you like to come?"

"Yes, of course," I answered.

I had been working with Rebeca one-on-one and had never seen her teach a class. It was amazing to attend her workshop, feeling peaceful and connected to God, angels, and the spirit world, with others.

"Close your eyes and imagine you are on a beautiful beach. Feel the sunshine, smell the salty air, and hear the sounds of the waves," she said, guiding us through the meditation.

The minute I closed my eyes, I heard a voice say "Mommy." I was standing on the beach and facing the ocean but couldn't see anyone there.

When the meditation was over, one of the women shared her vision, which was exactly like mine.

"I miscarried a long time ago. I have mourned for a long time. I know it's her, trying to contact me," she said, crying.

I had miscarried my first baby, too. Although I had grieved for a while, I had moved on with my life, not thinking about it since then.

I must talk to Rebeca later, I thought.

I saw Rebeca the next day.

"How was the experience for you?" she asked me.

"I had the same vision and feelings as the other woman in the workshop. It's interesting that I hadn't thought about that miscarriage in a long time."

"That is okay. Our loved ones stay close to us, even though we can't see or hear them. Let's do a guided meditation to learn more," she explained.

As soon as I closed my eyes and started the meditation, I felt the connection right away. "I can hear him. He is telling me his name is Daniel," I told Rebeca, tears in my eyes and overwhelmed with joy.

I also felt guilty that all those years my son's spirit had been with me, helping me like an angel, but I never thought about him. But mostly I was grateful.

"I can't describe the joy I am feeling in my heart and soul. Thank you so much for helping me to get to know my son, my little guardian angel."

I went home thinking about the wonderful experience I had, and I heard, "Mom, I love you."

This is one of the best days of my life. Thank you, God, and the beautiful heavenly angels, for helping me today. I will never forget this gift.

"Guys, come here," I called to the kids as soon as I got home. "I want to talk to you for a minute." I told them everything about my experience at the workshop and meeting with Rebeca.

"Mom, I think you have completely lost your mind," said Cyrus, laughing.

"I think it is very possible, Mom. Don't listen to Cyrus. He doesn't know anything." Azeeta accepted it very easily without any questions.

I continued my weekly sessions with Rebeca without telling any of my friends. I didn't know how to tell them without feeling embarrassed or being judged. It was a secret that only my children were aware of. Although it was hard for Cyrus to accept what I was doing, he strongly believed it was making me a better person. "Mom, you are a lot happier than before. I really love the person you have become." I noticed that I had changed too, feeling calm, relaxed, and happy.

Although I was satisfied and appreciated being able to communicate with my loved ones in the spirit world, such as my father, brother, and son, I was still searching to find more meaning and to learn about my purpose and mission in life.

"I still want to know the name of my guardian angel, Rebeca." I told her a week later. I was frustrated, having tried to learn this for a long time.

"Close your eyes and take a few deep breaths. When you are ready, try to visualize you are in a room, alone, and see a blackboard on the wall, right in front of you. Now, ask your guardian angel to appear and reveal his or her name," Rebeca told me.

The minute I looked at the board, I saw a picture of a beautiful red rose, and the name *Rose*, written in English and in Persian, appeared on the board. While still experiencing it, and with my eyes closed, I told Rebeca about the experience.

"Ask Rose to tell you how long she has been with you and what her message is today."

Before I asked the question, Rose showed me a time when I was four or five years old, in our old house in Iran. I was there with my aunt and my mother, wearing a white dress with red, yellow, and blue balloons on it. "Oh, my God, I remember that dress. My aunt made it for me, and I loved it very much," I told Rebeca. "I see myself, standing in the hallway right in front of the white refrigerator, looking sad. I remember my parents had an argument that night," I continued. "Rose is telling me that she was there, and she was trying to comfort me."

It was like watching a movie about my past, the part I didn't want to see. "I am sorry. I don't want to see anymore," I told Rebeca.

"That's okay. You are safe, Soodabeh. You can slowly open your eyes when you are ready."

Working with Rebeca was very exciting. I was making more progress every day, learning new and interesting facts about my life. I wasn't scared or frightened about what I might see at all, wanting to know more every day. Being able to communicate with angels and my family in the spirit world was comforting and gratifying. Rebeca would also give me messages from the spirit world.

"I have a message for you. The angels are telling me you are a healer," Rebeca said gently in one of our sessions, holding my hands.

"I had never thought my purpose in life was to be a healer. What does it mean, and what am I going to do?"

"You can help people heal spiritually by bringing comfort and peace to them," she responded with a gentle smile.

I then remembered a dream I had had several years before. I saw my father going on a business trip with my brother, Soson. I was very upset in my dream, arguing with both of them for not taking me. Soson looked at me and said with a beautiful smile, "It is not your time to go yet."

"Now, I know what he meant. It must be true—it's not my time to die yet. I have a mission and a purpose, to help those in need," I said, trying to explain the dream to Rebeca. "Wow, I can't believe I am a healer."

It is interesting when we have dreams about our loved ones who have passed, but we think they are still alive. We don't remember they have died, because they are alive in another place and dimension.

"How do I tell people I am a healer?" I asked Rebeca.

"All you need to do is to be aware of the gifts you have. God will bring people into your life, I promise. You have nothing to worry about, Soodabeh."

I was working the night shift, taking care of patients who were dying, in distress, and suffering in pain. Watching them gasp for air and hearing them moan, I wondered how to help them, since nothing had brought peace or comfort to them. I remembered what Rebeca had told me—"God will bring them to you"—and decided to try using my gifts for those patients. While I was checking them, such as taking their blood pressure, I put my hands on them and prayed for them.

"Please, God, let me be a clear channel to receive your loving and healing light and to help ease their pain."

I had no idea what could happen, but I was sure God was in charge and he knew what everyone needed.

One night I went to work and was assigned to a patient named Andrew. He had lots of pain after having a hip surgery, and he was agitated and in distress. Andrew had stopped breathing a couple of times and had been resuscitated and taken to the ICU, but he came back to my floor each time. Looking at him deteriorating was making me heavyhearted.

His wife was hurting, too. One day she came out of his room very frustrated and angry. She looked at me and said, "He used to be a very positive person, but now he has given up. I don't know what to do."

Andrew was very sick that night. He looked like a skeleton. His face was pale and gray, and he was moaning and grimacing constantly. I knew I had to do something to ease his pain. I decided to go see all of my patients first, before I saw him. I needed to have time to figure out how to help him.

I went back to his room, and after checking his blood pressure, I held his hands, closed my eyes, and started praying for him. I felt a cold sensation running through my body, from head to toe. Then, my hands became red and very warm, and my palms started tingling. I felt my fear vanish, and it was replaced by intense inner peace.

"Andrew, I know you can hear me. I am trying to give you healing energy, and I hope it brings you some peace and comfort. You have been suffering and fighting for a long time. It is time to go home if you wish, Andrew. Angels are here to help you."

Suddenly, I felt as if Andrew's spirit was coming out of his body. I panicked and opened my eyes, frightened of what I had seen, but I continued praying, holding his hands. Then I noticed he started breathing faster. His lips were moving, as if he were trying to tell me something, but no words were coming out of his mouth.

"Andrew, you don't have to say anything. I know you can hear me, and I am here to help you to see the angels. It is okay to go home with them. You are safe now, and will be in peace, soon." I stayed there until Andrew started to breathe slowly and stopped moaning.

"How is Andrew doing tonight?" asked one of the other nurses as I closed the door behind me.

"He was agitated earlier and in pain but he's doing okay and resting now."

I had told my coworkers I was learning about healing touch, and they had seen me reading books about the topic in my spare time.

Andrew's room was right across the hall from the nursing station, so we checked on him often.

"He seemed really quiet. Is he breathing?" one nurse wondered as she peered through the door.

"Yes," I said. "I really think it's the healing energy I gave him earlier."

I was off the next night and decided to light a candle before going to bed. I read for a while and then meditated and went to sleep. I woke up several times during the night feeling chills in my body and sensing a presence in my room. Every time I woke up, the bright light of the candle got my attention. It looked very bright, unlike any ordinary candlelight, as if it were shining with a heavenly glow. I knew I had had a visitor that night but never felt scared, and I fell asleep again.

When I returned to work two days later, I found out that Andrew had passed away the day after I had given him healing. I think the heavenly presence in my room that night was Andrew trying to contact me," I told Rebeca.

"You helped Andrew to die peacefully. He is here and saying thank you, loud and clear."

"I am very happy I helped Andrew go home and be in peace forever with God and the angels," I responded, feeling him right by my side.

It made me feel good to be able to help Andrew die peacefully and with dignity. I had trust in God and angels to help patients in need, but accepting and discussing the idea with others that I had the gift of healing was very difficult for me. Due to the lack of trust in my ability, I would question the messages and wonder whether they were from God or just my imagination. It was very hard for me to tell people about what I had heard or seen, thinking maybe it wouldn't be true. Consequently, I was still hesitant to tell my patients about it.

I decided to continue providing energy healing for the patients who were unconscious and likely to die within the next twenty-four hours. My intention was to ease their pain and suffering, make them comfortable, and assist them to transition peacefully to the spirit world.

Ruth was and very ill, and had been hospitalized many times. She was no stranger to me, since I had been assigned to take care of her several times before. Ruth was very strong and had been fighting the illness with every ounce of her being. She was one of the sweetest people I had ever known, always grateful for everything we did.

"Ruth, I love you very much. You are one of my favorite patients," I told her one morning right before going home.

"Oh, Soodabeh, you are the best, angel. I hope you will be able to rest today.

"I will be back tonight. I hope they assign you to me again. It's always great to see your lovely smile."

When I got back to work that night, I heard she had lost consciousness that afternoon.

"All of her family is here from out of town to say good-bye tonight," the charge nurse told me.

"Can I take care of her tonight, then?"

"Yes, I have assigned her to you. I knew you wanted to be there for her."

I went to her room right after I got the report. There were so many people in the room, more than I had expected. How did they all fit? More important, how was I going to do my job? I knew I had to find a way to be alone with Ruth.

"Could you please give me a few minutes to check her vitals? I would really appreciate it."

"Yes, no problem. You have to do your job. We appreciate everything you have done for her," Ruth's husband said before ushering everyone out of the room.

I took a deep breath and stared at her still body. *Thank God she is comfortable, at least,* I thought before checking her blood pressure. It was tearing me apart to let her go. I closed my eyes, put my hands on her chest, and started praying. I felt my palms slowly warming and tingling.

"Ruth, I know you have been fighting for a long time, trying very hard to stay here on earth. You will be safe on the other side, if you wish to go. Angels will guide and support you to go home, peacefully. I love you, Ruth, and I will always remember you."

I left the room with a broken heart but knew she would be in a better place soon.

"Thank you so much for giving me some time with her. Please let me know if you have questions or need anything tonight," I told her family before going to the nursing station to finish my charting.

It was five o'clock in the morning when Ruth's husband came and said, "Could we order some cereal and milk? Ruth just opened her eyes and is asking for cereal."

"She is?" I said, rushing to her room.

"Hi, Ruth. How are you doing?"

"I am hungry," she said, smiling, sitting up in the bed.

"I am glad you are okay. I will order it right away."

It was unbelievable for all of us to see she was conscious and awake, asking for food.

Ruth taught me a valuable lesson that night. I realized people only die when they are completely ready. The spirit is aware of whether it is time to go home or not. Ruth wasn't ready yet. In fact, she was discharged to go home with her family a few days later.

I told Rebeca about the wonderful experience I had with Ruth.

"I always thought when I gave healing to people, they would die. I never expected Ruth to prove me wrong."

"You need to remember that you are not in charge of knowing when someone is ready to transition to the other side. Spirit knows when it's time. We only die when it is the right time!"

I became more comfortable and confident, trusting God and angels to guide me to do the right thing. Knowing they were in charge of the whole process eased me into doing my healing work more often. I was fascinated by everyone's response to what I was doing. I would pray every night before going to work. *Please God, let me be your servant tonight, to channel your loving light and healing energy, helping those in need.*

One night I was assigned to John, a patient who was scheduled to have open-heart surgery in the morning.

"I don't think I am ready to have the surgery tomorrow. The evening nurse didn't answer my questions, and I don't know enough to make a decision," he said.

Both John and his wife seemed to be very nice people who were afraid of the outcome of the surgery.

"John, what are your questions? Maybe I can help you to decide, and if I can't answer them, I will call the resident on call to come here and talk to you."

He looked at me and said, "Well, I am concerned about the likelihood I'll die on the table."

"You have a choice and the right to refuse the surgery anytime, but do you have other options? What did the doctor tell you?"

"The doctor said I may not make it if I have another heart attack, and the surgery is the only option I have," John replied, looking at his wife.

"John, I lost my father when I was very young. He was the same age you are. I wish he could have had surgery and been here, but he could not. How do you feel knowing you may have another heart attack and die soon anyway, if you don't have the surgery? I know it is scary to go through an open-heart surgery, but believe me, I have taken care of lots of people older than you, and they made it."

As I was speaking to John and his wife, I felt my body language and voice change, as if an angel was speaking through me. I was speaking softly, in a warm and harmonious tone. I have always been very caring and sensitive to patient's needs, but that night I felt the loving and compassionate energy within my soul.

"I will be out there by the nurse's station. You both think about it, and let me know if you have any other questions. Would you like to talk to our on-call doctor?" I asked them.

"Thank you for all your help. We really appreciate it. I wish the evening nurse had spoken with us longer. I would like to talk to the doctor if it is possible," John said.

"Of course. I will call him right away," I said, and I left the room.

In the morning, I went to John's room. "What are you going to do?" I asked him.

"I have decided to have the surgery. Thank you for your effort, Soodabeh. I would have never agreed to have it done without you."

"You have made the best decision ever. I know you will be fine and very happy later. I will see you in a few days, then," I told him before leaving his room.

John was discharged a few days later, very happy and grateful to be alive. I knew it wasn't his time to die yet, and that was the reason God had sent an angel to help him that night. I was learning that healing happens in so many different ways, not just with me placing a hand on a chest and praying. It could happen with a smile, a tender touch, body language, and even with the tone of the voice. I didn't know how or when the healing would occur each time, but I prayed and allowed God and angels to work through me.

I believed and trusted I would be assigned to the patients who needed help.

One night, I was assigned to a very sick woman, Margaret. The doctor and her family had decided to make her comfortable and let her die peacefully. Her husband was sleeping at her bedside, and her son was resting on the reclining chair across the room.

I wish I could have some time alone with her, but I just don't have the heart to wake them up, I thought.

I decided to give her healing while checking her blood pressure, without waking up her husband or son. I put my hands on her arm and her chest and started praying silently. Suddenly, I felt as if an angel was inside of me, taking control of my every step. I was moving at the most harmonious, calm, and relaxed pace I had ever experienced in my life.

I had no idea her son was awake and watching me. After I gave Margaret a healing and right before I left the room, her son came to me, held my hand, looked into my eyes, and said, "Thank you for everything. There is something different about you, very kind and caring. Thank you for taking care of my mother."

"You are welcome. I am just doing my job," I said. I knew that his spirit noticed the presence of the angel with me, taking care of his mother. Margaret died the next day.

CHAPTER 19

I was learning to notice the changes and the way energy was being transmitted to the other person. I was grateful for everything I was experiencing; it was absolutely a miracle to experience this gift.

I was intrigued to learn more—things I had never thought were possible. I had begun to discover and believe in my gifts and my intuition, and I was more aware of the changes within my body every day. However, I wanted to do more and be able to see, hear, and feel exactly the way Rebeca was.

"I wish I was like you, the way you know and see things," I told her one day.

"But you are, Soodabeh, in your own way. We are different, yet able to feel, see, hear, the way it is comfortable for us. Also, it takes practice. The more you do it, the better you'll get," she replied.

"Thank you for the answer. But I still don't think I am as good as you are. I am happy that I can continue to learn from you, Rebeca. I trust you with all my heart and soul."

"Don't worry, you'll find out that you have the same ability I have. We are born with it, all of us. But, unfortunately, we forget these gifts, going through life, as we get older. You have to trust yourself. That's the only way you can be successful. I felt the same way when I started it, but I always trusted God and the angels to help me, and as a result, I began to trust my feelings as well," Rebeca said, encouraging me.

"I am feeling overwhelmed by the way everything is changing in my life. I grew up as an ordinary person. I felt invisible going through life, and now I am a woman with intuitive gifts to heal people," I would object.

"We all are the messengers of God, Soodabeh. This is our birthright. That is the reason you are here, so you can focus on your life purpose."

"I know, but I am scared of these changes and transformations at the same time."

Rebeca was so patient, listening to me, comforting me, and guiding me all the time. Although I would see Rebeca twice a month, I would call her every time I had a question about what I had experienced and ask for guidance.

My birthday was coming soon, and I was going to be forty years old. It was very important for me not to be upset or depressed, as I had been in the past. I wanted to celebrate every moment and enjoy life to the fullest.

"I want to do something unforgettable for my birthday," I told Rebeca. "It is a turning point in my life."

"It is very important to be forty this year, 2000, the beginning of a new millennium," Rebeca agreed.

A week later, Rebeca called me and said, "Rosemary Altea is coming to Sacramento in March. Would you like to go with me?"

"Of course! It would be the best way to celebrate my birthday."

I loved Rosemary, the renowned spiritual healer and medium, and *New York Times* bestselling author of *The Eagle and the Rose* and *Proud Spirit*.

A few weeks later, Rebeca and I stood in line to enter Rosemary Altea's workshop.

"This is so awesome," I said. "A new life, new job, and my birthday. I am so grateful for you, Rebeca, for mentoring and supporting me all the way."

"You are the one who did all the hard work, Soodabeh."

We entered the large room and saw about three hundred people. We listened to so many desperate people, but parents whose children had died had the most difficult stories for me to hear. I felt very blessed and grateful to have Rebeca to answer my questions. I didn't have to hope to be chosen from such a crowd.

"Rebeca, I feel so bad for these people," I whispered. "I changed my mind and don't want to have any messages. I only want some peace and comfort for these people.

"I know. They don't know how to contact their loved ones. I guess we are the lucky ones here."

"I can see Rosemary's spirit guide, Gray Eagle. He is standing right behind her," I told her with excitement. "Light and peace are everywhere I look. This is so amazing."

"Yes, I can see him and hear the messages, too!" she exclaimed.

It seemed as if she was the conduit of God's love and light, making it easier for both of us to see, hear, and feel better than before. I felt my brother and my father's presence stronger than I had ever felt before. We cried and laughed as Rosemary gave the messages to people. They were making it easy for all of us to believe in life after death, and with great humor at times.

Rebeca had bought Rosemary's book "You Own the Power" for my birthday, and after the workshop—while I was opening the book for Rosemary to sign it—I told her, "It is my birthday next week. Coming all the way from Portland was my birthday gift to myself.

Rosemary's beautiful blue eyes shined brightly as she met my gaze. I felt as if she was looking into my soul. And then she smiled.

"You are going to have a wonderful life," she said.

CHAPTER 20

I didn't know how the healing would take place or what I may say or do, but I trusted God's way. There was always a clue of some sort, something the patient would say to make me respond with an explanation of my healing ability.

"Wow, your hands feel so warm and nice. Thanks for massaging my legs. It feels so wonderful."

"You are welcome. I am glad you like how it feels. Do you know what energy healing is?"

"Yes, I do. One of my friends was telling me about the experience she had the other day."

"Well, that's why you felt the warmth of my hands. I have learned energy healing and love to help people whenever I can. I believe the energy doesn't come from me. It's God's healing energy running through my body and being transmitted to yours."

"It's wonderful. I wish more nurses were able to do this."

"I agree. The medical community is not quite open to it yet. But there is hope because of people like you."

It warmed my heart and soul to witness the joy, peace, and comfort people experienced as a result of my healing. I no longer had any fears of doing anything wrong, since I knew it wasn't my decision about who may or may not need a message or healing energy. There were times I didn't do or say anything to patients, knowing they weren't ready to discuss or hear the message, but even then I knew God provided whatever they needed.

After I gave healing energy, I witnessed patients being more open to listening and following the instructions about their health, and as a result, they would get better and would be discharged from the home health. I even experienced wounds healing faster than they should, which would amaze doctors and my coworkers.

"I can't believe your patients are acting so nice and listening to everything you say. When you are off, they miss you and can't wait to see you. How is it possible that our patients are different than yours?"

I would laugh and say, "I don't know. I'm just lucky, I guess."

I didn't know how to tell them about working with angels, in fear of being judged or misunderstood. However, eventually, after being questioned so many times, I decided to come clean and let them know about providing energy healing for my patients.

I knew I didn't have to talk about the power of energy flow with my patients. We are all made of energy, and people feel it whether they are aware of it or not. We all like and feel the positive energy of others.

I would wake up meditating and praying every day, asking for divine guidance to help me be a healing presence for others.

"Please, God, let me be an instrument of your healing light and energy."

Not only was I able to help people with their physical health but I also healed their emotional and spiritual wounds. Helping people with the healing light of God was making my life worthwhile.

I knew that was all I needed to do. It wasn't up to me to decide on whom to share the energy with; I simply believed those in need of the healing light and energy would be a recipient of it. My focus was to be of service to others by creating a sacred space for them to feel safe for healing to take place.

I had more patience and compassion for everyone and wasn't bothered or irritated by others' behaviors or actions. I was looking at life differently, learning to appreciate every moment. As a result of the changes in my life and attitude, everyone enjoyed interacting with me as well.

Getting rid of the old habits and replacing them with the new ones was difficult at times. I would go through periods of depression without any apparent reason, feeling sadness and despair.

The depression would happen as a result of the spiritual growth, Rebeca told me.

"Soodabeh, you have to learn to be patient and honor these feelings and emotions. Don't suppress them. Acknowledge and express your thoughts, knowing you are growing spiritually." I did learn to meditate more and read spiritual books when I was in that state of mind, and after a few days—once the depression had passed—I felt more sensitive and could feel, see, and hear better than before.

CHAPTER 21

I realized that every time I was feeling down or depressed, I was comforted by the presence of a loving spirit who held me at night until I fell asleep. It got to the point I was looking forward to the experience every night. Although I had no idea what or who it was, I sensed it was a male spirit. Each time I was visited by the spirit, I noticed a small red patch would appear on my face, forehead, cheeks, or chin, and it would disappear just as quickly. *Is this an allergic reaction to something I have eaten?*

I continued meeting with Rebeca twice a month, and we shared frequent phone calls in between. In one of our sessions, I told her about these new experiences. "I feel there are so many changes within me, and I can't keep up with them sometimes."

"Have you thought about past life regression?" she asked.

"I love to know everything, except about my past life," I laughed. "Maybe I was a criminal in my past life. I would rather not know about that."

One day, I was feeling very upset and irritable, experiencing one of those depressed moods again. It was a Saturday, and I was scheduled to work. There was a mistake in my schedule, and I wasn't happy about it. *That's all I need. I am not in a good mood, and now I have to stay here until I fix this mess before starting my day.*

I felt a male's presence, strongly, behind my left shoulder.

"I am sorry. I know you are here, but I don't have time to communicate with you today," I told the spirit.

"I really need to talk to you. Please listen to what I have to tell you," I heard him persist.

"Sorry, I am not in a good mood. I can't talk or listen to what you have to tell me. I have lots of patients today, and I am already late."

He followed me everywhere, tapping me on the shoulder. I whipped around as though he were a fly I could wave away.

It was a very long day, but finally I finished taking care of my patients and went home. I wanted to take a shower and go to bed right away, but my persistent friend from the spirit world wasn't about to give up at all. I had never felt so annoyed by any spirit before, so I asked him, "Could I at least take a shower before talking to you?"

After the shower, I went downstairs and lay down on the sofa in the living room. I started to meditate and pray for protection before communicating with any spirit, but my lovely friend started talking without my permission.

"My name is James, and I was your husband in a past life. I came to let you know I have always been with you and love you very much. When you are tired or down, I hold and comfort you. I know you have noticed that. For a while you thought it was your spirit guide, but it was me. I kiss your face sometimes. This is the reason for the redness on your face. We were in love, but one day I left you and never came back; I was killed in the war. That is the reason you can't fall in love. You are looking for the love we shared. Remember last year when you had a vision of coming down the stairs, wearing a beautiful evening gown, looking like a princess? You had a true vision of your past life, my love. We used to live in a castle, used to go to the balcony and talk forever. You have already had all these visions, and now you know they are true."

I was feeling very relaxed and loved. His presence was kind and gentle. He was kneeling right in front of the sofa I was lying on.

"What do you want from me now?" I asked him.

"I want you to acknowledge me, knowing I will always be with you, to love and protect you. I am coming back soon, mid-June. I will come and ask you to dance with me, and when you look deep into my eyes, you will recognize me." Then he kissed me good-bye and left.

I fell asleep shortly after, and when I woke up I felt so light, as if I had no worries whatsoever.

"See," Rebeca said when I told her about my visit, "you had a past life revelation, as a princess and not a criminal after all."

"Yes, I know. It feels good to know I was not a criminal in my past life, or at least in one of them!"

I kept thinking about the time I would see James, kept picturing what he would look like. James was the only thing on my mind. Feeling him holding me every night was very comforting. His presence was pure love; I had never felt anything like that in this lifetime.

I didn't tell my friends about James—they wanted me to have a real boyfriend, not a ghostly one—so they continued to encourage me to come out with them. Marsha called me one day and asked me to go ballroom dancing.

"I have been taking dance lessons at this place, and this Thursday is a free party. I was told we can bring guests. Would you like to go with me?"

Thursday was June 16th, mid-June. I agreed to go to the dance studio.

The place felt familiar as I walked in. "I remember I was here a couple of years ago with some other friends."

"You were?"

"Yes. I am not going to sign up for any classes, though," I told Marsha laughing.

"We are offering an introductory package tonight. You can purchase three lessons for only five dollars," exclaimed the young handsome guy in a black suit at the ticket table.

"Come on, Soodabeh." Marsha squeezed my arm. "If you buy this, I will get one free lesson. It's only five dollars."

"Okay, I think I owe you that much," I said. Marsha probably thought I was thanking her for getting me out there, but really was hoping to see my prince charming there soon.

My first dance lesson with the charming and very young Jack was fun. I laughed nervously throughout our session, especially when I couldn't even learn the basic step.

"I don't plan to sign up for more classes, Jack. This is it, so you better make me a professional."

"Sure, no pressure at all," he responded, laughing and shaking his head. "Do you like dancing?"

"Yes, I love dancing."

"Listen, you can continue dancing if you like. It's very simple; just like Marsha did, bring your friends with you. We have many promotions with the introductory lessons. Every time they sign up for the introductory lessons, you will get one free private lesson."

"You know, it sounds good to me."

I called some of my friends and asked them to join me for the studio's Fourth of July party. Jack had said there would be a drawing for free classes at that event.

"But I have never done ballroom dancing," said Teresa.

"They have a free group class and teach us how to dance."

"Okay, okay, I will go with you. Is Marsha going to be there too?"

"Of course, she was the one who encouraged me to go!"

I was very excited to be able to go there with some of my friends and have a great time.

At the studio, I was happy to see everyone having a great time. We were all laughing at ourselves, as we stepped on the instructors' feet.

"You know, Soodabeh," Jack said, "you can and you will learn to dance. But in the meantime, I am glad you are having fun stepping on my foot."

"I am trying, I promise. This is really hard."

"I know, but you have to let me lead. Stop being an independent woman, and let a man lead you once, please," he responded, laughing again.

"That's the reason I have been single a long time, I think."

It was the end of the class and time to announce the lucky winner of the drawing. I had so much fun and wanted to take more lessons.

"The winner is …" Jack paused and looking at the owner of the studio, Bill. "I am sorry, please excuse us for a minute," Jack said to us.

After a few minutes of discussion between them, Jack came back to the microphone. "Well, we normally don't do this. The winner has to be one of the students, not one of the guests with the introductory lessons. However, this time we are going to do it differently. So, the lucky winner is … Soodabeh."

I was shocked. "Oh, my God, I can't believe it. I have never won anything in my life."

"Well, this is our gift to you. I hope you enjoy and become a part of our studio," Bill told me. "You have won four private lessons and group parties. When do you want to start?" he continued.

"How about next week? I would like to take one lesson a week, if it's okay with you. I have a very busy schedule, but I would love to learn to dance better."

Everybody was amazed how lucky I was to win, considering I wasn't a regular student there yet. I couldn't even believe it myself, but I knew it wasn't a lucky coincidence. There was a very good reason, but nobody was yet aware of what it was.

I continued taking dance lessons with Jack and felt a special connection with him, although I knew it wasn't a physical attraction. We used to talk about everything while he was teaching me to dance.

"My mother is a nurse, too. She is like you, very independent, and raised me and my sister alone, without our father. I have a great respect for single mothers as a result."

"I see she has raised a wonderful young man. She must be really proud of you."

"Thanks. I am sure you have done a great job with your children as well."

One night when Jack and I started waltzing, I felt different. It seemed as if I was dancing with someone else, and as someone else. Although I was aware of the sensation of gliding on the dance floor, I had no control over my body. I was dancing like a professional, as if I had danced the waltz many times before, without any effort. I could feel pure love and harmony, dancing with the man I loved. I wanted to dance forever.

"Wow, Soodabeh," Jack said as the music ended. "Have you danced the waltz before?" "No. You must have taught me really well."

The strangeness continued with each dance lesson after that. I tried to explain it to Renee. "It's very interesting. One day Jack looks like my brother, Soson, and the next, I feel as if he is Daniel, the son I miscarried a long time ago. Sometimes he is this James, this long-lost love of mine."

"Jack must be a medium and has no idea what he is capable of."

"I am sure I am not going to tell him anything about it," I responded, feeling overwhelmed.

The next time I took a dance lesson with Jack, I felt the presence of an angel—not with him but with another instructor dancing nearby, Tammy. I didn't say anything and continued dancing. However, when Tammy came to say good-bye as I was leaving, without any plans to do so, I asked her, "Tammy, do you believe in angels?"

She looked at me and smiled but said nothing. I felt as if I had no control over my body again and said, "You know, I feel you have an angel on your left shoulder."

Tammy considered this. "I have a birthmark on my left shoulder."

"The spirit feels like a female, like a grandmother."

"My grandmother passed away last year."

"I communicate with angels, and that is the reason for the message."

We talked about the concept of angels and the spirit world for a while.

The next day, I went shopping and bought Tammy an angel statue and gave it to her before my next dance lesson with Jack.

Tammy, looking at the gift, said, "Last night I told my mom about what you said. My mom was very surprised and reminded me my grandmother passed away exactly one year ago from that day."

Jack came over and started asking me questions regarding the gift I gave to Tammy, but I didn't know how to tell him. I was judging him because he was a young man, and I thought he wouldn't understand me. I assumed he wouldn't have any interest in spirituality.

"I can't tell you, Jack. Could we start our dance lesson, please?" Jack didn't stop asking questions, wanting to know everything right then. "Could we dance first, please? I promise, I will tell you after the lesson."

"Okay, but I will not let you leave until you tell me why you got Tammy a gift."

I was very nervous about explaining it, but I was surprised to discover Jack was very interested and eager to hear and learn.

"Wow, Soodabeh," he said. "I have been praying for a teacher, and I would like to learn about what you do. Actually, I just gave my two weeks' notice. This is so strange but wonderful to know this about you right before I leave."

"What are you going to do?" I asked him.

"I don't know yet, but I know this isn't my life's purpose. I would like to have your phone number."

It was an amazing night. Angels had intervened not only to give a message of love and hope to Tammy but also to provide the opportunity for Jack to start down his spiritual path, answering his prayers for guidance.

In return, Jack allowed James to keep his promise and come to meet me in this life. I don't know if I ever would see James physically in this life again, but I cherish the memory and the pure, unconditional love we shared. It all happened because of Jack. And all of this started with a simple phone call from my dearest friend, Kim.

Being fully open and aware helped to change my life. All we need to do is listen to the guidance and follow the instructions!

CHAPTER 22

I woke up in the morning with an excruciating pain in my right wrist. I attempted to alleviate the pain by moving my hand and wrist in different positions but was unsuccessful. I got out of bed to take some Tylenol, but I couldn't even lift the bottle, let alone push and twist that child-proof cap. I walked to Azeeta's room and woke her up.

"What's happening, Mom?" she asked me.

"I don't know. I woke up and can't move my hand or wrist. I can't even change my clothes," I told her, crying.

"It's okay, Mom. Let me get up, and I will help you to get dressed."

I called my manager and notified her of my issue so I could go see the doctor.

She immediately figured it was something with a nerve and asked me questions about my job while wrapping my hand in a splint.

"It must be repetitive motions that eventually has caught up with you. It could be something simple, such as typing or taking blood pressure. How many hours do you work in a week?"

"I normally work eight hours a day, five days a week, but I have been working long hours lately, ten to twelve hours a day. I have spent many hours on the computer, documenting patient data and entering information."

"Well, there is your answer. I have worked with many patients who suffer from work- related injuries like this. Although it's common, it's hard to prove, unfortunately."

As she was explaining the cause of the pain in my wrist, I realized I had been neglecting myself, not taking time to rest and relax. Loving my job, I always thought I could handle it, not thinking it might not be good for me.

"Here, this is a prescription for the pain, and you can't go to work for at least a week. Make an appointment to see me next week. I hope you feel better soon," the doctor said.

My pain was lessening as we drove back home, due to the splint. "I don't know why I can't work for a week. My hand is feeling much better already."

"Mom, didn't you hear what the doctor told you? What happened to resting and taking care of your body?" Azeeta protested.

"I know, I know. It's just hard to sit at home and not do anything."

But I didn't have to worry for long about fighting my urge to work. The pain returned, and I couldn't take the pain medicine, since it made me drowsy and nauseated. I was frustrated that I couldn't even shower or get dressed. I prayed and meditated to feel better soon and be able to go back to work.

One week later, I went back to see the doctor, and she wasn't happy about the condition of my hand either.

"We need to start physical therapy for your arm and occupational therapy for your hand. Not sure when you can go back to work. We have to wait and see," she told me.

I was desperate to hear encouraging words, but there were none. My hand was getting worse every day. A numbness and tingling traveled up my hand to my elbow, then to my upper arm, all the way to my shoulder, and finally to my neck. My weekly trip to the doctor changed to daily visits to the neurologist, physical therapist, occupational therapist, primary physician, chiropractor, and massage therapist. And still there were no signs of healing.

Oh, my God, I am going to be disabled for life. What is wrong with me? And why can't anyone help me? Please help me. I can't live like this.

My right shoulder joined the pain club, and I was not able to move my arm at all, even after a cortisone shot.

"You may have a partial tear in your shoulder but not enough to have surgery," the orthopedist told me.

"What do I do now? I can't go through life feeling this way!" I said.

"I am sorry. I don't know what to tell you. But I am not willing to open you up and see there are no issues there. You need to continue with your therapy. Hopefully, you will get better."

Deep within me, I knew there was a reason I was not healing. One night, when I was meditating, I heard the message, "You need to start writing."

How can I write? I can't move my hand to do anything. But I heard the message again. "You need to start writing."

So, I took my splint off, got a pencil and paper, and said, "I am here and ready to write. Please tell me what I need to do, God. Please help me. I am very desperate for healing now."

To my surprise, the pain in my hand vanished suddenly, and I was able to write. It was unbelievable, but I was very excited about it. Angelic messages of hopes and inspiration ran through me, guiding me to what I needed to do to heal.

"You need to take care of your body and rest," I heard a voice say. "We have provided this time for you to learn, be a student, experience, and welcome this challenge. You will teach others later."

Being single and not having any other forms of income, I had to work hard to make money to pay the bills. Now that I felt more financially comfortable, I had started enjoying ballroom dancing, even getting ready for the dance competitions.

I was very happy and content with my life. Cyrus was happily married, and they had a one-year-old daughter. Azeeta was still living with me, working part-time and going to college. I was very grateful for all the blessings, especially my little angel—my granddaughter. I was happy and excited and never thought I needed to slow down and rest.

My hand started to get better very slowly after that night. I had been working with the same company for over ten years and had never been sick. As a result, I had accrued about two months of sick leave, but eventually all that time ran out.

"I have no more sick leave and need to go back to work," I told my doctor. "Could you please release me back to work? I promise to wear my splint between patients."

"I don't like the idea, but since you are a nurse and know what to do, I will let you go back to work. You have to continue with physical therapy, occupational therapy, going to the chiropractor, and getting massages several times a week after work," she explained.

I worked every day and took time to rest and relax every night by meditating and reading books. I decided to ask during meditation for the job I had always wanted: to work with an agency to incorporate holistic healing modalities in patient care, focusing on mind, body, heart, and spirit, rather than managing just the physical symptoms of the illness. I wanted to help patients to heal by teaching them how to take better care of their bodies, pay attention to their needs, and enjoy life. I knew it was possible, but I didn't know if any company like this existed.

Although my managers and most of my coworkers were aware I was practicing energy healing with my patients, it wasn't officially approved by the company. I wanted to be able to work with a company that provided these modalities for their clients, to help them heal, and to teach them how to live a healthy and happy life.

I started writing the requirements for my perfect job and the perfect company on pieces of paper and putting them in a box. Every night after meditation and writing messages from angels, I would come up with the things I wanted to manifest in my life, write them down, and put them in the box.

Being a nurse, I received medical magazines in the mail regularly. I usually threw them in the recycling bin without looking at them. One night, though, I collapsed on the sofa with the mail before going to the bin. The TV was on, so I was turning pages aimlessly at first, but then an unknown energy overtook my fingers, and I turned the pages with purpose. Before I could think, I saw a very small ad for the American Holistic Nurses Association.

Oh, my God, is this for real?

Filled with joy, I ran to the computer and found the organization. I signed up to be a member of the American Holistic Nurses Association right then. All I needed to do was, ask and wait for guidance. I knew I was about to experience another miracle in my life.

It was early December when I got my first issue of the association's *Beginnings* magazine. As I was reading every page carefully, I came across an article about a medical clinic in Washington that practiced healing modalities called "integrative therapy." I was beside myself. *Oh, my God, this is the job I wanted. This is the one I asked for just a few weeks ago,* I thought. I checked their website immediately and noticed they had a position available. I couldn't believe my eyes.

Still, I was in Oregon. *How am I going to do this? Am I willing to move to* Washington? I was confused and scared. *What am I going to do with my house? What is Azeeta going to do? How could I live without my family? Do I have to leave them behind for this?*

The answer was "Yes." Now I had to tell my family. I decided to go the "come right out and say it" route.

"I am moving to Washington," I told everyone after dinner.

They laughed and said, "We know you are sick and tired of Portland, but are you willing to leave us, especially your lovely granddaughter? Is this a joke?"

"No, I am serious this time. I have found a job already."

"What are you talking about? Where am I going to live?" said Azeeta, raising her voice.

"Well, you have two choices: to move there with me or to stay here. I am not going to sell the house, not yet. If you decide to stay, we can find a roommate for you. But if you decide to go with me, then I will rent the house. I am not sure how long I will stay there, but I need to go to learn what has always been my passion. I need to learn how this agency incorporates the integrative therapy modalities. Besides, as you know, I am sick and tired of this weather and need something different."

"Mom, if this is what you really want, we support you all the way," Cyrus said with a beautiful and gentle smile, although I could see he was sad for me to leave. "What are you going to do about missing your granddaughter?"

"I will visit at least once a month. It's only an hour flight. Maybe you guys could come and visit me."

Azeeta, on the other hand, wasn't ready to accept the change and cried constantly. It was breaking my heart to see her that way, but she was growing up and needed to experience being independent.

"I am sorry you feel this way, Azeeta, but you are twenty-one years old and need to learn to take care of yourself. You are going to stay in this house and will have a roommate. And you will have your dad, Cyrus and his wife, and all of your friends. They all love you and would do anything for you. I know it is the best plan for all of us."

But this logic didn't help Azeeta. She was sad and angry all the time. Looking at her, I thought maybe I should wait until she was ready. *Please God, tell me what to do. I want Azeeta be happy and safe here. Please show me a sign.*

Sally was my next patient. She was lying in bed, her nightgown disheveled, her blond and gray hair unkempt.

As we were talking about the history of her illness and the reason for her uncontrolled pain, she started feeling severe spasms in her legs and screamed in pain. I was astounded to watch her toes curl inward, and then her feet began to curl so that her toes were touching her heels. Without thinking, I reached down and touched her feet. To our surprise, her legs relaxed, and her feet went back to normal.

"What did you do?" she asked, staring at me.

"I practice energy healing sometimes, but this time I had no intention of doing anything. I was just shocked at how your feet spasm that way. It's not humanly possible."

"Thank God. At least you saw it. I have been trying to tell my doctors, but they think I am addicted to the pain medicine."

"I am so sorry you have to go through so much pain. I have been practicing energy healing and witnessed so many miracles. But this is the biggest one of all. I wish I could help you, but we are not allowed to incorporate it in our policy."

"I know. I have a friend who practices Reiki, but I have never felt like what I did today, when you touched me. I am very grateful for you."

"Why don't you try some relaxation techniques and see if it helps."

"Trust me, I will do anything. You have seen what I go through, and this is only one of my strange problems."

I gave her more energy healing before I went to talk to my manger, hoping she could be an advocate for bringing integrative therapy to our agency.

"I am sorry, Soodabeh. I have no power over management, but I will try my best."

Part of me knew that she wasn't going to discuss it with management, but I thought maybe, while I was waiting to hear the status of my application for the job in Washington, at least I could try here. I was hoping to have a chance to stay in Portland with my family, instead of moving.

When the timing was right, everything fell into place perfectly, just like magic, though I knew better. One of Azeeta's friends told her that she needed a place to live—what a perfect roommate.

I got a call from the manager of the agency.

"We liked your resume, and would love to have a face-to-face interview with you," she said over the phone. I was so excited and relieved they wanted to interview me that I called my friend, Marsha, to tell her the good news.

"Wow, I am so happy for you. I have a great friend there. Do you mind if I go with you? It would be the perfect way to celebrate your birthday together."

"That would be awesome!"

We left early in the morning and got to Washington one hour prior to my interview. Despite cutting the timing close, I was ready.

"Soodabeh, tell us what made you choose our company," said one of the nurses.

"I have always been passionate about integrative therapy and have been practicing energy healing, Reiki, and other modalities with my patients. Although my managers know about it, they don't know how to implement them as a practice. I saw an article about your company, and I am eager to learn how it is being incorporated here."

Seeing the approval in their faces and body language, I felt great.

"Marsha, I know I got the job. I want to go find an apartment today."

"Did they tell you that?"

"No, they said they will let me know. But I know they will hire me."

I had researched apartments online before I left Portland, and Marsha's friend and her husband were delighted to drive us around and show us the listing. The one that I had loved the most online was also the one I loved in person

"Nice find!" said Marsha's friend.

"It's all divine timing and intervention. I have many angels working behind the scenes!"

Soon the manager of the new company in Washington called to offer me the job.

"When are you available to work? Have you thought about which part of town you would like to live in?"

"I already rented an apartment. I can move there at the end of April."

"When did you find the apartment? I just called you!"

"Don't laugh, please, but the day of the interview, I had a gut feeling to rent an apartment."

"Wow, you are very bold, Soodabeh. I am looking forward to working with you soon."

CHAPTER 23

Azeeta helped me drive from Portland to Washington. It took us many hours, because we wanted to enjoy the drive, resting when we were tired or taking pictures of the magnificent scenery. We stayed overnight in a hotel and left early in the morning. The fronds of beautiful big palm trees danced in the air, greeting us as we entered the city. It was a magical day.

Azeeta was very excited to see all the beauty, taking pictures constantly and was happy I had found a safe place in the center of downtown, close to all the shops and everything I needed. "Oh, Mom, you did a good job. I may come and visit you more often." My little girl had grown up to be a wonderful lady and was looking after her mother!

"See, honey, I told you it is a beautiful city. I am glad you had a chance to come with me and see it for yourself. I know you have to work and go to school," I said.

"Mom, you went to school and worked while taking care of us. You know we will always be there for you, right?"

We got the key from the apartment manager and entered my apartment, a large one-bed room facing the courtyard with many palm trees. Sun shined between the leaves of the trees, passed through the sliding glass patio door, and spilled into the living room area, creating a warm scene. I was happy to have a great view to look at every day.

"This is really big and nice for you, since you have left your house to me to enjoy," Azeeta said, teasing.

"I know. Just don't have big parties in my absence. I can't come bail you out of jail. Besides, you know our neighbors are watching you," I told her, laughing.

"Oh yeah, me and my parties. You are the dancer in the family. So you don't be misbehaving now. We are busy and can't come here to bail *you* out of jail either."

When I returned from taking Azeeta to the airport the next day and saw the empty apartment, I felt lonely and vulnerable. *Oh, God, what have I done? Could it be possible that I have made the worst mistake of my life?* I believed I had followed the guidance of my spirit, trusting I would be happy, but that night I felt otherwise. *Please God, give me strength to survive without my family. I am scared and have no one to go to here.* I prayed before going to bed.

On my first day of orientation, I met the other nurses.

"Soodabeh, would you like to tell us about your experience as a nurse?"

"I have been a nurse for twenty-five years, working in many different health settings. I came here to learn about integrative therapy."

The others looked at me as though I was an alien. I could hear murmurs from some of them talking to one another.

"Did you come here only because of the integrative therapy?" one of the nurses said finally. "What is so special about the program that made you leave your family and friends to come here?"

I could sense the confused energy in the room, but I didn't care. I had to battle with management in other medical settings to allow me to use integrative therapy to help my patients, but they didn't.

I was excited to finally meet the director of integrative therapy, the one whose picture I'd seen in the magazine, with the article that had made me leave my family and friends.

"I have been working very hard to have this program approved and running," she said.

"I'm already impressed."

"I also teach at State University and different community centers. There are other opportunities coming soon, if you're interested."

I was thrilled to hear that I could be a speaker, but soon I received an even bigger opportunity. A few months later, Alice asked to meet me in private.

"Soodabeh, I am leaving the company. I am not sure when, but it will be soon. I wanted you to know, prior to announcing it. You are welcome to apply for my position. You are the only one who is really passionate about this program."

"Oh no. There is still so much I want to learn from you."

"When I started, there was no program or anyone to teach me. I had to implement programs. Some succeeded, and some didn't. It's great to learn by trying," she said.

By the time Alice announced her departure, the agency was going through a tough time. At first, they were going to consider someone to take her position, but they ended up laying off some employees, including some of the management positions and the director of the integrative program. Without a director, there could be no program.

I was so disappointed to have left my family and now to have to face this challenge.

Besides, there were different nursing rules and regulations in Washington. I had never thought it would be different working in another state, but it was. Considering I had many years of experience as a nurse, I hadn't gotten proper training.

I was frustrated, getting in trouble for not performing my job their way.

"But, this is how I used to do it," was my answer, which in turn would make everyone even more upset.

I was frustrated and unable to understand or figure out the difference. I cried when I would get home every day. I visited my family twice a month, and every time I did, I didn't want to go back to Washington.

"Mom, you know you can come back, right? Who cares what people may think? If you are not happy and so miserable, then you should come back to Portland."

"I am hoping things will change. I know there was a reason I was guided to go there. I can't give up yet, even though I am not happy there."

But after a year I decided to look for a job in Portland. I found nothing. *Please, God, help me. I am miserable here, miss my family, and have no one to trust. Please tell me what to do.*

The next day, my manager called me into her office.

Oh, my God, not again. What did I do this time?

"How are you doing, Soodabeh?"

"I am okay, trying to adjust and learn the system here, I guess."

"We are getting lots of letters from your patients regarding your professional behavior, your skills, the way you have been taking care of them, and educating them the way no other doctor or any nurse has done before. We are very pleased with your performance and happy to have you here."

"I am glad they feel that way. I am just doing my job. I love what I do, and I'm passionate about education and helping people recover from their illnesses. That's the reason I moved here."

"Yes, we know. I would like to know if there is anything I can help you to do, so you can do your job better, Soodabeh."

"Thank you. I appreciate it very much."

I realized then that God had intervened once more, answering my prayers and guiding me to stay longer to see the result. I knew it wasn't time to go back to Portland yet. *I need to change my view and learn the way they are performing. There has to be a way to compromise and enjoy this journey.*

One day, when I was at home meditating, I had a realization. *I need to accept and embrace my situation, be grateful for what I have and all I am experiencing here. This must be what I needed to learn, to be able to adapt to any situation, no matter how easy or difficult. I can't change others, but I can change the way I view things.* I was astounded to finally recognize the issue and find the solution.

The next day, I went to talk to my manager.

"I am trying to figure things out, and I believe I didn't have proper training. We all thought I didn't need it, and after three days of training, I started working solo. I know it will be easy for all of us if I can have some guidance about the rules and expectations regarding my position."

"I am so glad you came to me. I hope you know I love and adore you. I have been thinking about finding a way to help you. I know it must be very difficult to be away from your family, and I want to do whatever it takes to help you to enjoy your job."

As I changed my view of things, accepted my life, and did things the right way, I became happier and more satisfied. I stopped dwelling on what wasn't working and decided to embrace the beauty and life lessons around me. I cut back on my visits to Portland, so I didn't have to work as hard to make travel money, and I began to embrace my new home.

I started to go back to taking ballroom dance lessons, met wonderful people, and made amazing friends. Life was worth living again. As I became happier, I noticed my intuition increased more, and I was able to help others more, especially my patients.

One day in the staff meeting, one of my coworkers discussed an issue he had with some of his patients.

"I know Alice is gone, but we have some patients in desperate need of integrative therapy. I don't know what to do," he said.

"Well, Soodabeh has been doing integrative therapy and came here mainly for the program. We could always give her a referral and ask her to do a consultation. Is this okay with you, Soodabeh?" said the director of the nursing program.

"I will be more than happy to."

"I didn't know. Is Soodabeh replacing Alice?" one of the nurses asked.

"No, we don't have a position for the integrative therapy anymore, but we are grateful to have Soodabeh here."

"Well, not everyone knows about this. Is there any way to make sure all the nurses and therapists have this information?"

"I'll email everyone that she's available."

A few weeks later, I got a phone call from the director of the nursing program to meet her.

"I have heard great things from your colleagues about your consultations and helping their patients. The monthly orientation for new employees is coming up, and I was wondering if you could spend some time then explaining the integrative therapy program."

I couldn't believe my ears. "I would be honored," I answered.

"You earned the opportunity. I was also asked by the director of public relations if you would like to participate in some of our fundraising activities in the community."

"Absolutely. That would be a dream come true. Thank you so much."

I was thrilled to be a speaker and have workshops to raise awareness about integrative therapy. Our agency was once again the agency in the area providing an integrative therapy program for patients. Over the next few weeks, I became a preceptor and trained the new nurses, and then I was asked to partner with a prominent physician in the area to create a program to help patients with multiple illnesses and difficult-to-treat cases. As a result of the hard work of all the dedicated and professional nurses and therapists, our agency was recognized as one of the "Elite Agencies" in the area!

I have many heartwarming and touching stories to share. The integrative therapy modalities work, and I am one of many medical professionals who attest to that. Learning about integrative therapy not only helped me to be a better and healthier person but also it helped many patients claim their right to having happy and healthy lives, in spite of the challenges of facing health issues.

I was able to witness the effectiveness of utilizing integrative therapy. It keeps patients out of the hospital and emergency rooms, allowing them to stay happy and independent at home, and it leaves more money to be saved for the agency.

It may take a long time to see this practice accepted and utilized by health care agencies nationwide, but I will always cherish the wonderful memories of helping my patients transition peacefully or claim the right to live healthy and happy lives. Meanwhile, I continue serving clients in my private practice, doing what I love—helping people succeed, enjoy life, and be happy and healthy, no matter what their conditions or circumstances are.

We can help people by providing the right tools, skills, and education to manage their symptoms. We are not bound by our circumstances; we can be happy and content even though we have an illness or face a challenging situation.

PART 3

HEALING WITH ANGELS

CHAPTER 24

Though I was enjoying the magnificent scene out of the car windows as I drove—the rays of sun shining between the green, yellow, and orange leaves of the beautiful tall trees—and admiring what God had created, my mind was split. It was also thinking about Mary, the new patient I was going to see. I was praying that everything would go smoothly, but I was doubtful it would.

I had called Mary the day before to make an appointment for our first visit.

"Come in the evening," she had demanded.

"I work from 8:00 a.m. to 5:00 p.m. and since the first visit can last up to two hours, we need to start no later than 2:00 p.m," I said. I felt frustrated right away, because of her tone.

"But I have other plans in the daytime. I have a guest coming to visit me."

"I am sorry, Mary, but as I said, I can't see you later than 2:00 p.m."

"I don't know what to tell you, but I can't do it earlier."

"How about the next day? Could we postpone the visit to the next day, please?"

"Yes, I guess," Mary responded abruptly and hung up the phone.

Mary had breast cancer, and it had spread to her bones. This was the end. My heart was aching for the woman I didn't even know. And I feared she would not be easy to make comfortable.

When I got to Mary's house, nothing looked as though there was someone so sick inside. Beautiful red, pink, and yellow roses greeted me as I walked to the red wooden door. I took a deep breath and rang the bell.

"Come on in," said the man who opened the door. He had a beautiful, friendly smile. "I am Jack, Mary's husband. She is waiting for you in the living room."

I followed Jack along a narrow hallway to the living room. I sat on a sofa across from a fireplace. On my left, Mary reclined in a light brown chair. Her frail body and pale face made her appear older than sixty.

I could feel the tension in the air. Mary was knitting something with beautiful light pink and yellow yarn but not making eye contact with me.

"What are you making?" I asked.

Shrugging, Mary put the knitting on the wooden coffee table in front of us, reached over to pick up a book, and showed me a pattern. "It keeps me busy. I used to be very active, but now I don't have any energy and get tired easily."

"I am sorry to hear that. It must be very difficult for you. When did this start, Mary?"

"I was diagnosed with breast cancer eight years ago. The doctor did a double mastectomy. I was fine until a few months ago. I thought the cancer wouldn't come back again," Mary said with tears in her eyes. She was trying so hard not to show any emotions and be strong, but I could feel the anger and frustration in her voice and eyes. I had seen it before. I was searching really hard to find any trace of light or hope in her eyes, but I couldn't. I knew it would be very challenging to bring back life and light to those beautiful green eyes.

Jack came into the living room shortly. "Honey, do you need anything?" he asked Mary.

Looking at him, Mary said, "We have been married for twenty-five years. Poor Jack thought if he married someone a lot younger than him, he would be happy. Look at him—he will be eighty years old next week, and he looks younger than me." Jack smiled and just looked at her without saying anything. It was breaking my heart to see how sad he was.

"I had chemotherapy once a week, but it made me very weak. I couldn't tolerate the side effects. I had nausea, couldn't eat, felt fatigued all the time, and was just miserable."

"I am sorry, Mary. You have gone through so much. No wonder you don't have any energy left. Do you have any pain?"

"Yes, I have severe pain in my right leg. I have been on continuous intravenous pain medication, but the pain hasn't been controlled."

"I am planning to visit you twice a week, making sure your pain is under control," I explained. "We can also try a combination of guided imagery, relaxation techniques, and energy healing. What do you think, Mary?"

"I am open to trying anything, as long as it relieves my pain."

I left the house, praying. *Please God, help me to ease her pain.*

Each time I visited Mary, she appeared a little worse.

"Mary, you need to eat more. Can you at least drink some milkshake to get some energy?" Jack begged her one visit.

"I can't, honey. I have no appetite, and I will vomit if I even look at food," Mary responded. To me, she said, "I can't even leave bed now. I am so frustrated and hopeless."

As time went on, Mary did seem more comfortable around me, finally able to express her feelings openly. During one afternoon, I was sitting on a chair right by Mary's bed documenting the details of our visit. Suddenly, Mary sat up, looked at me, and said, "When is it going to be over?"

I looked at her and responded, "What do you mean, Mary?" Although I knew exactly what she meant, I wanted her to open up. I closed my computer and sat beside her on the bed.

"I mean ... I am tired," she said, gasping for air. "This pain ... is making me ... miserable. How long ... umm ... do I have to ... suffer? I am ... really tired and ... want to ... die."

I put my hand on her shoulder and then wrapped my whole arm around her, bringing her closer to me. "You will die when you are ready. It is your decision. You will know when it is time."

She wiped her tears and said, "Have you been there? I mean ... have you been there when ... umm ... someone dies? What does it ... look like? How do ... they feel?"

"Yes, I have been. They look very peaceful. We always make sure they are very comfortable. I believe when someone dies, angels and their loved ones in the spirit world come to greet them, to make their transition a pleasant one."

As I was telling Mary about the angels, her breathing slowed.

"I think I need to lie down, Soodabeh."

"Okay, let me help you."

She took a deep breath and closed her eyes. She looked very relaxed with a smile on her face before falling asleep.

The following week, Mary was hospitalized for surgery to have a device implanted in her stomach that would deliver adequate pain medicine. But the surgery, in addition to staying in the hospital and still enduring chemotherapy, made Mary weaker every day.

On my first visit with her after she returned home, I thought she looked like a skeleton.

However, Mary was a very strong and determined woman. She wanted to feel better and was motivated to do whatever it took to get out of bed. Her fight gave the device time to work, and her pain became more controlled. She was able to eat without feeling nauseated. I believe the twice-weekly healing energy and relaxation techniques were working to her advantage as well.

I usually called Mary in the morning to tell her that I would be there in the afternoon.

"Can you come after 2:30 p.m. today?" she asked once. "I have an appointment with my hair dresser today."

"Why don't you go see her and enjoy your day? I will see you tomorrow afternoon," I responded.

The next day, I was pleased to see Mary looking refreshed and very beautiful. She was very excited, showing me her short hair with blond highlights. The old, gray color of her face had been replaced by a pink one, and her beautiful blue eyes shined with light.

"Wow, you look stunning, my dear," I told her.

"I am going to die gorgeous," she responded, laughing.

"What do you mean?"

"I decided to stop chemotherapy yesterday. I don't know what happened. We were at the doctor's office, and I suddenly told him that I was miserable and want to stop the chemo. It came as a shock to Jack and the doctor. To be honest with you, I don't even believe the way I said it. I just knew that I didn't plan it."

"I support you, Mary. You made a very important decision, and I am very proud of you. I knew you would know the right time to do so."

As we were talking, my coat fell off the sofa, and I heard, "The angels are here, and they have a message." I smiled and bent down to pick my coat up. Then, I heard the front door open, but when I looked, no one was there. I heard again, "Angels are here, and they have a message."

I closed the door, put my coat on the sofa, and sat beside Mary. Looking in her eyes, I said, "Mary, angels are here, and they have a message for you. They are telling me that your journey going home will be very comforting and peaceful." Mary reached for my hands and burst into tears. I continued, "They are promising they will be here to take you home when you are ready."

She looked so calm. She had been fighting to survive for others, and had forgotten her own emotions. Now that she stated her feelings and been validated in them, she felt at peace.

"What is next, Soodabeh?" Mary asked.

"I think it's time to sign up with hospice."

"Will you be my nurse still?"

"I am afraid not. But I promise, you will be in good hands. They have wonderful and trained nurses."

"No, I don't want it then. I don't want anyone else but you." It took awhile for Mary to trust me, and it would be difficult for her to get used to a different nurse at this point.

"Mary, you know I love you very much, but I can't provide what you need anymore. But I will visit you twice a week still, talk with you, give you energy healing, and visit as a friend."

"Okay, as long as you promise to visit me, I will sign up with hospice," Mary agreed.

I usually saw Mary on my way home. It was easier for me that way, because I could stay there as long as I wanted and she needed.

It was the end of November, and during one of my visits, Mary gave me a gift—a beautiful black scarf with red and green flowers on it. "This is one of my favorites, Soodabeh. I want you to have this and to always remember me."

"Oh, I am so honored to have this, and I will love wearing it."

"I only have one wish, to stay here until after Christmas. I hate to put my family through the pain of losing me before Christmas. I just can't do that," said Mary.

"I am praying for that, Mary," I said. "I have to share something with you. I have been thinking about writing a book for so long, and I finally signed up to take a writing class."

"What is it about?" she asked.

"The story of my life challenges and healing with angels. Do you mind if I write about you?"

"Not at all. You have helped me so much, and I want everyone to know about your skills and the way you help others. I am pleased to be a part of your book."

I was off work the last day of writing class, and I woke up late feeling really depressed but didn't know why. I had an appointment to see Renee that day, and when I got there, I told her about how I felt.

"Don't worry—this is going to pass. Just take some time to rest and relax. You must be tired from working so much."

I went home and finished my final paper on Mary. I was excited to share the story with my classmates and teacher.

"It's such a powerful and touching story, Soodabeh. Thank you so much for sharing this with us," my teacher said.

I had been working for a long time, making sure to have the best story to share, and I felt very proud to have it done so on time.

The next day, when I went to work and checked my messages, I heard a voice mail from Mary's daughter.

"I wanted to let you know that mom died yesterday morning. I wanted to thank you for all the wonderful work you have done for her and our family. She loved you very much and always looked forward to your visits. Thank you for helping her relax and go home peacefully."

I burst into tears and knew the feeling I had had the day before was Mary letting me know of her journey home.

Mary still visits me sometimes, helping me when I am in a stressful situation and providing care for other patients. I know one day we will meet again, and she will be one of the angels to come and greet me to take me home. May she rest in peace!

CHAPTER 25

I was on my way to go see Julie, a new patient with a history of heart disease. She had been in the hospital for a long time after open-heart surgery, and after she was discharged she was very anxious, calling every day and night, complaining about having shortness of breath and afraid she might be having another heart attack.

I parked my car on the gravel road by her house and entered the yard through the small gray gate.

One of the caregivers opened the door, smiling. "Please, come on in. Julie is waiting for you."

As I entered the narrow, dark hallway, I saw Julie lying on the sofa. There was a bed right across from the sofa, with another caregiver sitting there. I was surprised to see two caregivers for only one person and was looking forward to find out the reason.

"Hi, nice meeting you, Soodabeh. I have been waiting for you for a few days now," she said, sitting up slowly. She looked pale and tired.

Looking at her shoulder-length silver hair pulled back in a ponytail and her deep blue eyes, I noticed beauty and wisdom behind her sickness. I sat on the sofa next to her.

"Feel free to let me know when you are tired and want to rest," I said. I wanted to make sure she would be able to tolerate the visit without compromising her heart.

"I used to be very active, going sailing, rafting, traveling, and doing all sorts of outdoor activities," she said, smiling. Her face fell. "But now I am constantly worried that I'll have another heart attack.

That's why I have these young ladies to take care of me. One of them is in charge of the cooking and housekeeping, and the other one sits here and makes sure I am okay and breathing. I am really scared, Soodabeh."

Julie had to stop talking frequently to catch her breath. I held her hands, trying to give her energy healing to help her to calm down and relax.

"We have a program called integrative therapy, using relaxation techniques, guided imagery, and energy healing to help you to relax, if you are interested, Julie."

"Oh, I will do anything. I am constantly nervous. I didn't like to stay in the hospital and don't ever want to go back there again. I used to drive before this, but now I am even scared of walking by myself."

"I am sure you will be able to get better soon and back to normal. I would like to see you three times a week for the next few weeks, then down to twice a week, and when you are ready, I will visit once a week before discharging you. What do you think?"

"Just hearing this plan is making me feel better already."

"Okay, then. I will see you in a few days. Meanwhile, I would like to try some deep- breathing exercises with you. Don't try hard, only what you are able to tolerate. I want you to do this exercise with your caregivers a few times a day, especially before going to bed. Do you listen to music?"

"Yes, I like classical music."

"Perfect. Put on the music and try to take a deep breath, hold it as long as you can, try for the count of three to five, and exhale. That's all you need to do for now. Do you think you can do this?"

"Yes, I will give it a try."

"This may seem simple, but it's very effective," I told her.

Julie was a very intelligent woman, but she was just scared. She was not used to this kind of life. I knew teaching her some relaxation techniques would help her bounce back soon.

I called Julie to make an appointment to see her the next day. "How are you doing?" I asked.

"I did really well last night. We practiced the deep breathing exercises and I had a great night. I can't wait to see you again. I want to show you something."

When I got to Julie's house, she was sitting on the sofa looking refreshed and excited.

"I wrote a book many years ago, and I want to show you." She picked the book up off the coffee table and put it in my lap.

"Wow, this is amazing. It's wonderful to see your book." Really, I was excited she was back to thinking about her life in happy terms rather than fearful ones.

"What would you like to work on today?" I asked. "How about I give you different exercises today. I have a CD of ocean sounds. What do you think about that? Knowing that you used to sail and raft, could that work?"

"Yes, let's try that." She looked at me with a genuine smile on her face.

Julie was getting physically and emotionally stronger. I was amazed by her strength and determination to do whatever it took to get better. There were no more phone calls to the office, so everyone was happy.

"Even my appetite is getting better, Soodabeh," Julie said one day. "You are really good at what you do. How come no one else told me about this service before?"

"Well, unfortunately, they don't teach these techniques in nursing school or medical school. I started learning these techniques to help myself to get better, but now I am planning to teach it to my patients as well. That is the reason I moved to California, since this agency is the only company that incorporates these techniques to help their patients."

"You know, I was wondering if you could check my blood pressure and heart rate before and after these relaxing techniques."

"That's a great idea. Let's do that today."

I checked Julie's blood pressure, heart rate, and the oxygen level prior to the relaxation technique, after ten minutes of the deep-breathing exercises, and again once we were all done.

"Yes, it worked!" said Julie, looking at her measurements.

"Thanks to you, we now have scientific proof."

I worked with Julie for a few weeks before we started working on guided imagery.

"I want you to close your eyes and listen to the music, breathing slowly. When you are ready, imagine you are in your favorite boat and sailing. Feel the cool air, the sun is shining, and you are content, enjoying the day." I could see all the muscles in her face relaxing. At the beginning, I would lead her through the guided imagery and relaxation techniques, but after a few weeks she became more independent.

Julie was getting better every day, not only with the anxiety but also all aspects of her health—her heart, lungs, and appetite had improved. "I have even noticed hair growing on my scalp. This is absolutely amazing."

"I am so happy for you, Julie. It was definitely a pleasure to work with you. You should be proud of yourself for being motivated to take time to do the exercises. You are the main reason for the improvement."

"Since I have been feeling better, I have decided to have only one caregiver. I will be more independent and able to live alone soon."

"Wow, this is amazing."

"Yes, I think so. I really appreciate everything you have done for me. As a matter of fact, I wrote a letter to the director of the nursing services in the hospital, requesting their nurses to be trained by you. I wrote to her that every hospital needs a *Soodabeh*. They all should know there are ways to help people to have a great life, in spite of the illness or health issues they may experience."

"Yes, I agree with you. This is my dream that every medical institute incorporates the integrative therapy modalities. They are not difficult to teach, yet they are very effective and could save lives."

Julie became independent by using the relaxation techniques, feeling stronger than ever, and began to drive her car again. I was very grateful and honored to be a part of Julie's recovery!

CHAPTER 26

I was approached by one of my colleagues about a young patient in her early thirties suffering from multiple sclerosis. She was having a lot of issues with pain, and none of her medications had relieved it. She was losing her independence and was frustrated, since the medical world was not able to address her issues.

I was praying that God and the angels could help me to assist Monica. I had had great results with patients with neurological disorders, so I was hopeful I could help her as well. I parked my car in the driveway, climbed a few cement steps, and rang the bell. Monica opened the light brown door and invited me in. She was petite, four ten, barely a hundred pounds, and fragile. She walked ahead of me, dragging her left foot across the hardwood floor, and asked me to have a seat on a chair at the dining table.

"Thank you for coming to see me. Would you like a cup of tea or water?"

"No, thanks. How are you doing, Monica? Tell me about your condition, please."

While showing me her deformed fingers, she said, "I have been suffering from rheumatoid arthritis for many years. Unfortunately, I was diagnosed with multiple sclerosis a few years ago. It has been very debilitating and painful for me to do anything. I can't drive, do any household chores, or even walk without pain."

"What have you been taking for pain so far?"

"Unfortunately, I can't take that much pain medication. My body is very sensitive, and I have allergies to most of them. The one I can take makes me very drowsy and unable to function mentally during the day. So, I usually don't want to take anything, which leaves me in a state of constant pain."

"As you may know, we always rate the pain level from zero to ten—zero meaning no pain and ten being severe pain you can't tolerate. What is the level of your pain now?

"It is definitely an eight."

"I am going to start with some relaxation breathing exercises, and give you energy healing. Is this okay with you?"

"Sure, thanks."

"Please close your eyes and take several deep breaths to relax. I will stand behind you and touch your shoulder to provide the energy healing. You may feel the warmth in my hands or even experience a sensation of energy flow where I touch you. Please let me know if anything makes you feel uncomfortable or creates more pain," I explained.

I kept talking to her while providing energy healing, making sure she was comfortable. After a few minutes, she said, "You are right. I can feel your hands getting warmer. It feels really good and comforting. My whole body is relaxing, and I can feel the warm energy flowing all the way from my shoulders to my ankles and feet."

"Great, just make sure to take deep breaths. The more you breathe and relax, the more energy flow you will experience."

"I have never experienced anything like this, Soodabeh. How do you do that?"

"I pray to God and angels to take over my body. It's like plugging in an electronic device, such as a television or a computer, into an outlet. That's how I channel the energy from heaven. This is the reason you feel the change in the temperature of my hands."

As I provided energy healing for Monica, I got messages to guide me to move my hands along her body—her neck, spine, hips, knees, ankles, and feet. It took me about thirty minutes.

"What is your pain level now?" I asked her.

"My pain has decreased to one or two. This is incredible."

I felt overwhelmed with joy and gratitude. I had left my family to live there, alone, to follow the guidance of my spirit. Although I was missing my family, especially my three- year-old granddaughter, I was happy to be serving God and heaven, bringing healing light and energy to those in need.

I went to see Monica again the following week, and she had good news for me.

"Soodabeh, I can't believe it, but my pain was between two and four all week. I have never been so comfortable, being able to move around freely.

"I am so glad I could help. Let's start our session, then."

Monica made progress slowly but steadily, and after each visit her comfortable feeling lasted longer than before. She learned she was not stuck with pain and discomfort. She had all the tools she needed to have a happy life, even though she had multiple sclerosis.

CHAPTER 27

I was about to see Jack, a young man suffering from multiple sclerosis. He had been confined to bed for a very long time, almost twelve years. He couldn't talk, eat, or do anything for himself. He lived with his wife and mother, and they were very supportive, taking care of all his needs.

Although it is very sad to have such a debilitating disease, he was lucky to have a dedicated mother and wife to take care of him.

Jack's wife, Samantha, greeted me when we arrived—really, she and the couple's two yellow and chocolate Labradors greeted me— and led us to Jack who was lying in bed, smiling but otherwise quiet and still.

What wasn't quiet was the large and loud ventilator whooshing and humming to the left side of the bed, a machine designed to mechanically move breathable air into and out of Jack's lungs, since he was unable to do so. A long white tube connected his windpipe to the ventilator.

To the right side of the bed, an IV pole with a small bag filled with brown liquid, a nutritional supplement, was connected to the gastric tube, which had been surgically inserted into his stomach since Jack was unable to swallow.

Seeing Jack so dependent on his wife and mother made me feel very sad and heavyhearted. I started wondering what his life purpose could be, questioning God's will—the reason Jack was alive and living that way. Looking at his young wife and mother, who had taken care of him for twelve years, I admired both of them for loving Jack and accepting him the way he was.

While watching him and talking to his family, I saw a flickering of light in the hallway out of the corner of my eye. I thought it was my imagination. Then shiny stars formed all around Jack's head and shoulders.

I was speechless, watching this wonderful phenomenon right before my eyes. I felt no control over my body, and all of a sudden my mouth opened, and I said, "I see angels around your head and shoulders, Jack."

Everybody looked at me.

"They are here to protect you and your beautiful spirit, Jack. This is their message for you."

Tears rolled down Jack's wife and mother's faces, and the joy this message brought to them was clear. I realized God had answered my question about Jack's purpose and mission in life by showing me all the angels with him and protecting his family in their journey. I knew I had witnessed unconditional love. That was Jack's mission.

"I am so sorry I blurted that out about the angels. I am a healer and have no control when there is a message for someone. I hope you are okay with this."

"Oh, my God, Soodabeh. I have been pondering about the reason for living like this for a while," said Jack's mother. Your message warmed my heart and gave me the courage and the answer to know we are doing the right thing. It made me appreciate life and what we do. Thank you so much for the message."

Jack's family was very protective of him, but when they found out I worked with angels, they had no objection to me working for them. I was fascinated by the way people would accept and trust me, welcoming me into their homes.

CHAPTER 28

I was to go see another patient, Helen, who was suffering from chronic heart and lung disease. She had recently been discharged from the hospital and needed a nurse to make sure she was being cared for at home. I called Helen's daughter, Jan, and notified her of the time of my visit.

I arrived at her house, parked my car on the street in front of it, and walked toward the brown wooden gate. I opened the pale green wooden gate, entered the yard, walked toward a glass sliding door, and rang the bell.

"Hi, my name is Soodabeh, here to visit Helen."

"Yes, I'm Jan. Come on in."

I stepped past Helen's daughter, following her extended arm to see an old woman sitting by the dining table. She was bent forward, head in her hands, looking very frail, and her face was dusky due to her heart condition and poor oxygen in her cardiovascular system. Her long gray hair was pulled back in a ponytail. Helen answered my questions with her eyes closed.

As I was sitting there, listening and writing, I felt as if someone was pulling my chair back. I looked back, but I didn't see anything. I pulled the chair closer to the dining table and continued with the conversation, trying to document everything. A few minutes later, I felt the same sensation; my chair was being pulled back. This time was more obvious, making me jump. I tried to cover my strange action by laughing as I said, "I could swear someone was pulling my chair back."

Jan looked at me and said, "Oh, it is my dad. He has a good sense a humor."

I knew from Helen's records that Jan's father had died a few months earlier. I matched her calm tone. "Thanks for telling me. I thought it was my imagination." If she was surprised that I wasn't surprised, she hid it; we laughed.

"I do energy healing, working with angels, and the spirit world." I continued. "I am happy to be able to experience this, and it doesn't scare me." I felt honored for being greeted by a spirit with a great sense of humor.

"He only plays with those who have a good sense of humor, are sensitive, and are aware like you," Jan responded with a beautiful smile.

It was quite an interesting visit, unlike any other, as we openly discussed God, angels, and the spirit realm. They told me about Jan's father, Helen's husband, the wonderful man, who endured so much and died peacefully and with dignity.

"Have you read any interesting books lately, about all of this?" Jan asked as she showed me to the door at the end of the visit.

"Actually, my favorite book is *The Proud Spirit* by Rosemary Altea. It is an amazing book for you to read. Rosemary works with an American Indian spirit guide named Gray Eagle. I could loan it to you the next time I visit."

"Oh, sounds great." Jan said. "How often do you come to visit Mom?"

"Twice a week for the first few weeks, since she is very sick, but then once a week. We can always change the frequency depending on her condition."

"I'm sorry we need you, but I am looking forward to speaking with you again in a few days, then."

The feeling was mutual.

Helen's condition was worse every time I saw her, but the visits were very special, as I witnessed all the love and respect of Helen's many children and grandchildren, all of them very caring and attentive to her needs.

"It is an amazing experience to come here to visit you, Helen," I told her one day before giving her energy healing. "It is an honor to be at your service. You and your family have brought so much love and joy into my life, and I will appreciate and cherish it forever."

"Oh, Soodabeh, you are very sweet. Thank you for the energy healing. It has been making me relaxed and less anxious. I have been able to sit and enjoy my family without falling asleep so much."

Still, Helen's overall condition was deteriorating rapidly. It was very hard for me to see her fighting patiently.

Finally I said to Jan, "We have done everything we can."

I knew I had to prepare Helen for her transition. I prayed God would give me the strength to accept her condition and help her to be as comfortable and peaceful as she could be.

Once Helen had become unresponsive and unable to communicate with us, I spoke to her. "Helen, I know you can hear me. You have been fighting for your family. Angels are present right now and ready to escort you home, safely and peacefully. You can join your husband and the rest of your family in the spirit world. They are all waiting for you, Helen," I told her silently while I was giving her energy healing. I left her home with a heavy heart, knowing I would never see her again.

The next day, I got a message on my answering machine at work regarding Helen's transition. I burst into tears. Although it was expected, I still had a hard time letting go. Helen and her family had become part of my life, and it was as if I had lost one of my family members. I cried all day trying to be calm at each patient visit, but the minute I would get in my car, I would start crying again. I knew I had to visit Jan and the rest of her family.

"Hi, Jan, this is Soodabeh," I said over the phone. "I was wondering if I could come to see you later this evening."

"Yes, please. We would love to see you."

The minute I saw Jan, we fell into each other's arms, and we both cried for a while. It was very difficult for us to calm down. But, finally, when I was able to sit down and able to talk, I told Jan about my last visit with Helen.

"Your father was waiting for her with many angels. He asked me to tell her he was looking to see her soon. I am sorry. I didn't know how to tell you, but I had to tell Helen."

"We knew it too. Thank you so much for being a part of her life and making her comfortable. At least she wasn't in any pain or agony and died very peacefully."

CONCLUSION

Life is full of challenges. There are lessons to be learned and experiences for the spirit to grow. We are spirit in human forms, chosen to come to this earth to learn and enjoy life to the fullest. The journey may not always be easy, and could be very challenging at times, but we have to be willing and ready to learn the lessons.

Be kind and gentle to yourself. Be patient and love yourself and others. Take time to enjoy life, rest, relax, and have fun. Miracles happen every day, but sometimes, we are so busy, we can't even notice them. The simple acts of being able to see, hear, smell, walk, talk, and eat are miracles. We take everything for granted until it's taken away from us.

I am no exception and used to take life for granted, but now, every day, I wake up trying to pay more attention to all the blessings in my life and to be grateful for everything, no matter how big or small. Even in the face of challenges, I remind myself of the miracles I have witnessed. Learn to appreciate life, everything you have, and embrace the good, the bad, and the ugly.

Life is too short. I have witnessed that every day, taking care of my patients and clients, and also by losing my loved ones, family members, and friends. Stop the pain, the guilt, the shame, the anger, and the resentment. Forgive yourself and others, be grateful for the lessons, and look for all the possibilities that are available for you right now.

We have free will to decide what we want and which direction to go. We are in control; we have the power to change our lives and destinies. God has created angels to help us, but we need to ask. So, be ready to ask, believe, take a leap of faith to follow the guidance, and be open to experience the miracles!

Love, light, and blessings ...